ROUNDL

Also by Jon Stallworthy

POETRY
The Astronomy of Love
Out of Bounds
Root and Branch
Positives
Hand in Hand
The Apple Barrel
A Familiar Tree
The Anzac Sonata: New and Selected Poems
The Guest from the Future

ANTHOLOGIES
The Penguin Book of Love Poetry
The Oxford Book of War Poetry
First Lines: Poems Written in Youth, from Herbert to Heaney

EDITED
Wilfred Owen: The Complete Poems and Fragments
The Poems of Wilfred Owen
Henry Reed: Collected Poems

AUTOBIOGRAPHY
Singing School

BIOGRAPHY
Wilfred Owen
Louis MacNeice

LITERARY CRITICISM
Between the Lines: W.B. Yeats's Poetry in the Making
Vision and Revision in Yeats's Last Poems

TRANSLATIONS
(with Peter France)
Alexander Blok: Selected Poems
Boris Pasternak: Selected Poems

JON STALLWORTHY

Rounding the Horn

Collected Poems

CARCANET

First published in 1998 by
Carcanet Press Limited
4th Floor, Conavon Court
12-16 Blackfriars Street
Manchester M3 5BQ

A CIP catalogue record for this book
is available from the British Library
ISBN 1 85754 163 4

The publisher acknowledges financial assistance
from the Arts Council of England

Set in 10pt Garamond Simoncini by Bryan Williamson, Frome
Printed and bound in England by SRP Ltd, Exeter

Contents

A poem is / 11

from THE ASTRONOMY OF LOVE (1961)
Romance / 15
Song at the Turning of the Tide / 15
You not with Me / 16
Boy and Fox / 17
The Master-Mariner's Epithalamion / 18
Letter to a Friend / 19
Poem upon the Quincentenary of Magdalen College / 20
A Dog's Death / 22
Still Life / 22

from OUT OF BOUNDS (1963)
Out of Bounds / 27
First Blood / 28
Miss Lavender / 29
No Ordinary Sunday / 30
War Story / 31
Climbing Parnassus / 32
Traveller's Choice / 36
After an Amputation / 36
Letter to my Sisters / 36
From W.B. Yeats to his friend Maud Gonne / 38
Toulouse Lautrec at the Moulin Rouge / 39
The Assault / 40
The Trap / 41
Sindhi Woman / 42
Camel / 43
In the Street of the Fruit Stalls / 44
The Face / 44
First of the Migrants / 45
Last Post / 45
The Swimming Pool / 47
Tent-Pegging at Night / 48
'Here comes Sir George' / 48
The Peshawar Vale Hunt / 49
Cowboys / 50

Bread and Circuses / 51
Quiet Wedding / 52
Witch's Sacrament / 52
Feet off the Ground / 53
Green Thought / 53

from ROOT AND BRANCH (1969)
For Margaret and Geoffrey Keynes / 56
A True Confession / 57
The Postman / 58
A rose is not a rose / 59
A Barbican Ash / 60
Sensation / 61
Telegrams / 61
An Evening Walk / 62
As Others See Us / 63
Harvest Moon / 64
Two Hands / 64
Thistles / 65
The Stone / 66
False Alarm / 67
Firstborn / 67
By Rule of Thumb / 68
The Fall of a Sparrow / 69
At Take-Off / 70
On the Road / 70
Epilogue to an Empire / 72
Kathmandu-Kodari / 74
A Prayer to the Virgin / 74
War Song of the Embattled Finns / 75
Sword Music / 76
A Portrait of Robert Capa / 77
A poem about Poems About Vietnam / 78
T.E.L. / 79
A Word with the Baas / 80
A Letter from Berlin / 82
Elm End / 83
Old Flames / 85

from HAND IN HAND (1974)
A Bottle of Ink   /   91
Elegy for a Mis-spent Youth   /   91
Words on a Paper Tablecloth   /   92
Walking against the Wind · /   93
Positives   /   94
After 'La Desserte'   /   98
Pour Commencer   /   99
So Much in Common   /   99
The Source   /   101
A Question of Form and Content   /   101
Daybreak with Horses   /   102
Breakfast in Bed   /   102
Personal Column   /   103
A Pair of Gold Dolphins   /   103
Message Received   /   104
African Violets   /   105
Homecoming   /   105
Picnic   /   105
The Play of Hands   /   106
Willow-pattern Blues   /   106
Through a Glass   /   107
A Dinner of Herbs   /   108
The Last Word   /   109
In the Zoological Section   /   109
Again   /   110
The Beginning of the End   /   110
Making an End   /   112
Apollinaire Trepanned   /   114
Burning the Stubble   /   114
In the Park   /   115
Resurrection   /   116
The Writing on the Wall   /   117
Mother and Child   /   118
At Bedtime   /   118
The Almond Tree Revisited   /   119
This Morning   /   119

A FAMILIAR TREE (1978)
At the Church of St John Baptist, Preston Bissett   /   123
  ENGLAND
Mother and Son   /   124
Old John Young John   /   125
To the Honourable Members of the House of Commons   /   126
In the Name of God Amen   /   128
The Birds o' the Parish   /   129
William   /   131
To Samuel Greetheed, Evangelist, Newport Pagnell Chapel   /   132
News From Home   /   132
Patchwork   /   133
The Tuscan   /   134
  THE MARQUESAS
The Departure   /   136
The Arrival   /   136
The Beginning   /   137
The Contest   /   138
The Trials   /   139
The Return   /   143
  NEW ZEALAND
Mother and Son   /   145
The Arrival   /   146
A Proposal   /   147
A Prayer   /   148
An Expostulation   /   148
With a Copy of *Early Northern Wairoa*   /   150
A Couple of Field Postcards   /   150
Congratulations   /   151
The Return   /   152
  ENGLAND
Home Thoughts from Abroad 1939   /   154
Home Thoughts from Abroad 1955   /   154
Identity Parade   /   156
The Almond Tree   /   158
One for the Road   /   162
Envoi   /   163

THE ANZAC SONATA (1986)
Counter-Attack / 167
One Day / 167
The Rooms / 168
Defying Gravity / 169
The Blackthorn Spray / 169
Mother Tongue / 172
The Anzac Sonata / 173
At Half Past Three in the Afternoon / 180
Frozen Poem / 181
Winter was a white page / 183
Windfalls / 184
Making a Table / 184
For Zhenia Yevtushenko / 186
For Margaret Keynes / 187
In Memory of Geoffrey Keynes KT / 188
Goodbye to Wilfred Owen / 190
Wiedersehen / 190
At St Gennys / 192
Great Britain / 193

THE GUEST FROM THE FUTURE (1995)
The Nutcracker / 201
The Girl from Zlot / 210
The Guest from the Future / 219
The Voice from the Bridge / 227
From the Life / 231
The Thread / 235
The Naming / 237
The Women / 238

Notes to *A Familiar Tree* / 239
Index of First Lines / 243

A poem is
something that someone is saying
no louder, Pip, than my 'goodnight' –
words with a tune, which outstaying
their speaker travel as far
as that amazing, vibrant light
from a long-extinguished star.

THE ASTRONOMY OF LOVE
(1961)

Romance

Why, when my head was filled
with maidens for whose sake
kings sold their castles, headsmen felled
a forest of tall princes, and
the woodcutter's sons were drowned in the lake;

why, when my heroines
sang Te Deums from the rack;
from faggots rampant at their shins;
or, tossed between sea and sand,
elbowed the lighthouse dinghy to the wreck;

why should I look, not once,
but ever since, answer me that,
at you with no falcon or lance
but a basket in your hand,
and, for a crown, your least heraldic hat?

Song at the Turning of the Tide

O do not let the levelling sea,
the rub and scrub of the wave,
scour me out or cover me
with sand in a shallow grave.

But let my image, like a rock
contemptuous of the tide's attack,
shift no inch at the green shock
and glisten when the wave springs back.

You not with Me

Walking – but you not with me – round
a glass sky fallen into Blenheim lake,
I see the wind's invisible dancers waltz
from hill to water, and the cloud-floes break
superbly into swans. And I
who know what songs the fields are singing, drowned
in their green wave, know that the singers lie.
The rooks trumpet for summer on a false
alarm. Else why should you, my swan,
be restless to move on?

Our inward weather does not take
its season from the year. Below that beech
once in a roaring month we could not see
leaves dancing like the damned, nor heard them preach
warning of winter. All that day
the skeletons wore green again, the lake
stole colour from your eyes. Long as you lay
between my arms, the wide arms of the tree
would let no leaf, or squall, or wing
intrude upon our spring.

So long as April weather filled
the heart, we lived the poems of our love
without restraint of intellect or rhyme.
Just to perfect the living was enough,
when all along the avenue
and in the hedge we saw the small birds build:
and though no bird in all that summer flew
nearer to heaven's lake, when had we time
in the astonishment of spring
to stretch the throat and sing?

The ancient serpent, tooth in tail,
now stirring at the centre of the world
turns also in the heart. A season ends,
and love's tranquillity at last is thrown
into the violent ditch. I see

16

our reason bending to the body's gale
and stripped as naked as the beaten tree.
Naked I am: but safe from crossing winds
of love, my white bird disappears
against a squall of tears.

May you in this migration find
summer beneath your wings, as when we brushed
a winter's slate sky clean. Till you return
no spring can rustle in the blood, now hushed
and frozen with a final kiss.
Over the desolate waters of the mind
the storm advances. Gathered into this
upon the dark lake's darkest edge, I learn
it is the breaking of the wing
teaches the swan to sing.

Boy and Fox

Little fox, little fox, with your brush of hair,
I have carried you everywhere
all day against my skin. I said
no calloused hand shall rub the head
I fondle, nor shall curious eyes
explore your body like gross flies.
Jump up, and you shall keep me warm.
How could I guess that you would worm
your muzzle through my ribs, and tear
tissue from bone as if your lair
lay in my stomach? From the wound
my heart bangs like a sail in the wind
about to split with its own thunder.
Split heart, and spill your thunder.
Little fox, work on, and gnaw
every root to the red core
until, drum-bellied, you lie down
curled in a cavity of bone.

Then let us sleep and think we know
a kinder consummation. Now
from the Spartan I would learn
to joke and whistle in the lane
louder than the nagging teeth:
but how shall I conceal beneath
the white stare of this face, this shirt,
the creeping colour of my hurt?

The Master-Mariner's Epithalamion

There was a captain who, weary of land,
called for his swallow-tail coat and cravat,
his buckle-shoes, spyglass, and tricorne hat;
and called on deck a thumping band
to stuff the sails. From bollard, quay,
and painted hulls,
a squall of gulls
blew him over the switchback sea.

Twelve days out in the roaring lanes
a mutinous crew beat down his door.
Some he pistolled on the cabin floor,
marlin-spiked the bosun's brains
and clapped the deck-hands into irons;
but at his back
on every tack
pounced the sea like a pride of lions.

There was a helmsman, too intent
on a lunatic compass ever to feel
his fingers broken by the snarling wheel;
over whose head the waters went
and the whip-thongs of torn sail.
Night fell, and the mast
splintering, passed
pennoned into the jaws of the gale.

Flamboyant signals of distress
erupted from his hand: but dark rain blocked
the golden rain, and tongues of lightning mocked
each muzzled rocket. Rudderless
through all the angles of the chart
his vessel drifted,
till an iron wave lifted
and, falling, cracked its timber heart.

There was a castaway, who shook
a captain's coat in the wind's teeth, gave
his buckle-shoes to the tug of the wave;
who risen out of the wreck –
see! – naked as a dolphin swims
into the humbling,
surf-white, tumbling,
sanctuary-harbour of your limbs.

Letter to a Friend

You blame me that I do not write
with the accent of the age:
the eunuch voice of scholarship,
or the reformer's rage
(blurred by a fag-end in the twisted lip).
You blame me that I do not call
truculent nations to unite.
I answer that my poems all
are woven out of love's loose ends;
for myself and for my friends.

You blame me that I do not face
the banner-headline fact
of rape and death in bungalows,
cities and workmen sacked.
Tomorrow's time enough to rant of those,
when the whirlpool sucks us in.

Turn away from the bitter farce,
or have you now forgotten
that cloud, star, leaf, and water's dance
are facts of life, and worth your glance?

You blame me that I do not look
at cities, swivelled, from
the eye of the crazy gunman, or
the man who drops the bomb.
Twenty years watching from an ivory tower
taller than your chimney-stack,
I have seen fields beyond the smoke:
and think it better that I make
in the sloganed wall the people pass,
a window – not a looking-glass.

Poem upon the Quincentenary
of Magdalen College

The chapel silent and the candles weeping.
White boys erect, each with the sun
alive beneath his skin and gold blood leaping,
stooped in one hour; were levelled soon
with the arterial weeping of despair
into old men. Although a lifetime slips
through this night's sorrow, none will shift his stare.
Their beards shake white below the fluttering lips,
their hands still tremble in the stress of prayer.

They weep because no guests will mourn with them
the dying of five hundred Junes.
Tongued bells are dumb: the requiem
sleeps in the organ's throat, and tunes
swirl only on the tented lawn. No psalms
are scrolled in smoke above the shadow pall,
but for this night, freed from a mason's charms,

the stone musicians tip-toe from the wall
with tabret, lute, and viol in their arms.

For one not lit with eyes the pipers blow
nothing but silver, fiddlers weave
a tent of scarlet with the shuttle bow.
What more should he believe
beyond the kiss of taffeta and shower
of heels? Like shells that toll for their bell-tongued seas
his ears ring back the changes of the hour.
He only understands the prophecies
of iron pigeons gathering in the tower.

It seemed he whistled as the night was failing
a dirge for unremembered years,
and on his face the moth-winged rain was falling
persistent as the candle's tears;
and neither priest nor prophet turned his head
for whirling girls or laughter from the crowd.
These saw the Great Tower gilded: they instead,
through the sarcophagus, through mask and shroud,
saw naked the dimensions of the dead.

Now morning shovels in the sunlight, bringing
a blackbird in the last tail-coat
to raise the requiem. He stills us, singing
in the small chantry of his throat
the song the blind boy whistled through the rain.
The dancers all have dwindled into stone,
the mourners given up their ghosts of flame.
Tabret and lute and kettle-drum alone
in carven hands upon the arch remain.

A Dog's Death

This dying of the dog, now gone to earth
in some abandoned catacomb of the mole,
confronts us with our shadows. In that hole
lies a boy, dead, and crouching by this hearth
a man's dark image. Always I can feel
his hand on mine. We loved the dog, but banish
his name, his basket, and the painted dish,
to shake the clinging shadow from our heel.

As on so many evenings when we set
the last of the china zodiac on its shelf,
the dog would bustle to the door and bark;
in this hushed kitchen I cannot forget
how, at the dropping latch, I would myself
enter the moonblaze or the howling dark.

Still Life

A feature of the guest-house window
like the cracked pane and the shrivelled fly,
she drops no stitches if the lap-dogs bark
or flinches when a bus throbs by.
She who is nobody's wife or widow
sits, like a furled umbrella from the hall,
watching the boys play cricket in the park
and powerless to retrieve their ball.

With a knitting-needle quill all day
she writes the latest chapter of her life
for grandchildren, not hers, to stretch and pull,
rough-handle till it fray. They would not laugh
at the loose hand so readily, if they
could read the breaking heart between the lines.
Pity and terror fit her parable
for the grey language of the skeins.

She does not, like the house-maid, hear the clock
have hourly palpitations on the wall.
She does not hear the chauffeur's double knock
and the jolt of the chest in the hall.
Through the cracked window-pane leaks in the dark
until it seems she scarcely breathes at all;
watching the boys play cricket in the park
and powerless to retrieve their ball.

OUT OF BOUNDS
(1963)

For Richard Sorabji

Out of Bounds

The world was flat, lawn without end,
when first we left the house. Later we stood
at the world's edge over a newfound land
dizzy with orchards. These and the tall wood
contained us for six summers; meadow and
wilderness a seventh. Then we found
the fence that proved the world was round.

We broke out over the dead
limb of a larch and in the Colonel's park
trespassed till supper, trespassed all that year.
Emerging once from the wood's cathedral dark
we saw miles off, but every sail-rib clear,
a windmill standing at ease, its head
laurelled with small, bright clouds. We said,

'We could do it in half a day.'
The sun was in mid flight. Down the first hill
bracken stampeded with us, cantered up
the second, ambled up the third. The mill
like a schooner from wave top to wave top
whenever we closed seemed to veer away:
nautical miles between us lay.

Minute by minute the sun burned
down like a rick into red ash, fading
to grey, then charcoal. We were gaining now
on a giant in seven-league boots, wading
thigh-deep, head-down over seas of plough
and plunging grass, who as we looked lurched, turned
back; and the darkness churned.

Like skeletal arms the black
sweeps gestured to the sky. One field to cross;
another to go round; a stile; we went
stumbling between tall hedges, and there was
one field more. As if by common consent,
with hardly a word spoken, we turned back
shoulder to shoulder down the track.

Afterwards we said, 'Another time
we will start earlier', but though we went
many fields further, north, south, east and west
of the windmill, by that same consent
we left it undisturbed. Though I have crossed
mountains and seas since, I have yet to climb
a hill not seven miles from home.

To climb for what? To find a grey
skull, lichened, cobweb-raftered, with the wind
a ghost lamenting through its broken teeth?
Better to leave the features undefined
than rob the landscape of a last wild myth.
Still the sweeps signal in my head: are they
beckoning, or waving us away?

First Blood

It was. The breech smelling of oil,
the stock of resin – buried snug
in the shoulder. Not too much recoil
at the firing of the first slug

(jubilantly into the air)
nor yet too little. Targets pinned
against a tree: shot down: and there
abandoned to the sniping wind.

My turn first to carry the gun.
Indian file and camouflaged
with contours of green shade and sun
we ghosted between larch and larch.

A movement between branches – thump
of a fallen cone. The barrel
jumps, making branches jump
higher, dislodging the squirrel

to the next tree. Your turn, my turn.
The silhouette retracts its head.
A hit. 'Let's go back to the lawn.'
'We can't leave it carrying lead

for the rest of its life. Reload.
Finish him off. Reload again.'
It was now *him*, and when he showed
the sky cracked like a window pane.

He broke away: traversed a full
half dozen trees: vanished. Had found
a hole? We watched that terrible
slow spiral to the clubbing ground.

His back was to the tree. His eyes
were gun barrels. He was dumb,
and we could not see past the size
of his hands or hear for the drum

in his side. Four shots point-blank
to dull his eyes, a fifth to stop
the shiver in his clotted flank.
A fling of earth. As we stood up

the larches closed their ranks. And when
earth would not muffle the drumming blood
we, like dishonoured soldiers, ran
the gauntlet of a darkening wood.

Miss Lavender

Miss Lavender taught us to ride
clamping halfcrowns between saddle and knee
on Sunday afternoons
in a watermeadow one mile wide:
and the hot halfcrowns
she would keep, after an hour, for her fee.

Her horses stepped like a king's own
always to imperatives of Spanish drill.
Miss Lavender said,
'A horseman has to be thrown
ten times.' From thoroughbred
to exploding grass we headoverheeled; until

that March the watermeadow froze
and Miss Lavender died, consumptive
on a stable floor
among motionless horses. Those
died after for no reason, or
for want of a Spanish imperative.

No Ordinary Sunday

No ordinary Sunday. First the light
falling dead through dormitory windows bl
with fog; and then, at breakfast, every plate
stained with the small, red cotton flower; ar
sixpence for pocketmoney. Greatcoats, line
by the right, marched from their pegs, with
poppy fires smouldering in one lapel
to light us through the fallen cloud. Behind
that handkerchief sobbed the quick Sunday

A granite cross, the school field underfoot,
inaudible prayers, hymn-sheets that stirred
too loudly in the hand. When hymns ran ou
silence, like silt, lay round so wide and deep
it seemed that winter held its breath. We he
only the river talking in its sleep:
until the bugler flexed his lips, and sound
cutting the fog cleanly like a bird,
circled and sang out over the bandaged ground.

Then, low voiced, the headmaster called the roll
of those who could not answer; every name
suffixed with honour – 'double first', 'kept goal
for Cambridge' – and a death – in spitfires, tanks,
and ships torpedoed. At his call there came
through the mist blond heroes in broad ranks
with rainbows struggling on their chests. Ahead
of us, in strict step, as we idled home
marched the formations of the towering dead.

November again, and the bugles blown
in a tropical Holy Trinity,
the heroes today stand further off, grown
smaller but distinct. They flash no medals, keep
no ranks: through *Last Post* and *Reveille*
their chins loll on their chests, like birds asleep.
Only when the long, last note ascends
upon the wings of kites, some two or three
look up: and have the faces of my friends.

War Story

of one who grew up at Gallipoli
not over months and miles, but in the space
of feet and half a minute. Wading shoreward
with a plague of bullets pocking the sea
he tripped, as it seemed to him over his scabbard,
and stubbed his fingers on a dead man's face.

Climbing Parnassus
For Dick Watson

I
Between
the olives' grey and green
silver-combed sea
and the cliff Parnassus, Delphi.
Between
the amphitheatre edge
and the stadium, we
asleep along a ledge
between
a pomegranate awning
and the rock.
Between
moonset and morning
six o'clock.
Up vaults Apollo
astraddle
the mountain's saddle,
filling the hollow
valley with the clatter
of light.
Where olives break like water
foaming grey and white
around Apollo's temple,
pillars tremble,
pavement stones ignite,
and marble walls unfold
a rose of sudden gold.
Now seven men like copper moths,
after much writhing, crawl
from eiderdown cocoons
sealed with a dream of myths
into a waterfall
of goat-bell tunes.

II
Giving the god a flying start,
two of the seven strip and cool
their faces in the Muses' pool;
plunge; towel their shoulders till they smart;
take their breakfast and depart.

Entering soon the stadium,
its terraces now like the wreck
of some giant fossil in the rock,
imagination knocked us dumb.
As if a dinosaur should come

alive, the broken skeleton
put on its flesh again. The crowd
stood on their seats, chanting aloud
our names. What could we do but run
into the long straight and the sun?

Two shadows turned into the bend:
many shadows swept out: and we,
deafened with silence suddenly,
were jostled sideways by a wind
that overtook us from behind.

III
We followed then the track Apollo blazed
with thistles like diminished suns,
remembering unremembered Greeks, who gazed
on such a morning up the mountain once;

artists and athletes like the charioteer
of sea-green bronze, whose sandles pressed
stadium sand and thistle-track here,
clambering, wing-heeled, to the mountain's crest.

Laughter blew back to us, arguments flapped
in our faces, and we shared the joy
of some, it may be, that the javelins dropped
like bursting sacks among the stones of Troy.

You spoke of Wordsworth in the Alps, and I
of Owen in the Pyrenees;
young men awaking under such a sky
as we woke under, climbing tracks like these;

and finding among mountains day and night
a revelation of delight,
altered perspectives, and an infinite
curve of landscape swinging into sight.

Here spirits grow. They travel up as trees
to meet the sun, (roots tunnelling
for foothold on the slope). The wind makes these
its instruments and, at its touch, they sing

in darkness how the migrant bird of day
approaches. Some, standing so tall,
are singled out by lightning: even they
illuminate the forest as they fall.

Smaller than wrens, higher than any lark,
not until half the climb was done
and shadows crossed our shadows, did we mark
the eagles poised between us and the sun.

IV
Apollo raced us to the top
and would not stop
to share the bread and cheese we broke
on our sky-surrounded rock.
Parnassus under us, we lay
under the round sky all the day
with the round world at our feet
vibrating, pulse-like, in the heat:
and were content to know
there was no higher place to go.
Pan, in a shepherd boy's disguise,
screwed up his wicked, winking eyes
and piped away our afternoon

with so incomparable a tune
that ancient goats about his feet
capered like midges in the heat.
All roads led round and up to this
candle-flame of consciousness
within a hat's round shade; and where
would lead, how should we guess or care?

V
Words we abandoned on the downward climb:
each, like Aladdin in the enchanted cave,
cramming his eyes with wealth. It was a time
when heaven was an unflawed turquoise, save
where in the west the bullion-smelting sun
poured ingots of bright gold; and southward one
of silver, where the gulf's shock-headed wave,
curling, uncurling, up the inlet ran.

Apollo swings out of his saddle. Far
below, the petals of his temple close.
Turquoise turns amethyst, and one sharp star
of the first water, at the moon's throat, glows.
So, often from the crags of sleep, I come
downhill to Delphi, supper, and the hum
of friends around that fire: when in my nose
no tripod smoked and oracles were dumb.

Traveller's Choice

Counsel yourself that traveller
who in a fiery desert found,
when half starved for water,
a well-shaft glimmering in the ground –
no rope or bucket to be had
and the sweet water twenty foot down –
should he crouch in the heat and go mad
or plunge into coolness and drown?

After an Amputation

After an amputation, he had heard,
the patient feels his missing limb
foreshortened, still a part of him
but like a snail's horn shrinking; and his hurt
more of the truncheon than the knife.
The surgeons did their work. Through life
the ache persisted, somewhere between heart
and head. His boyhood every day
crept closer as he moved away.

Letter to my Sisters

Asleep till nine, again you break
your croissants by the tideless lake
where small fish quarrel for crumbs
and, making with its paddle-beat
no more stir than a swan's feet,
the day's first steamer comes

obliquely to the landing stage.
At ten you walk into the village
for the long hot loaves and cheese
to be eaten as you lie
halfway to a Renaissance sky
among the crocuses and bees.

As my days have been, your day is.
Cowbells and churchbell and the kiss
of scythes in tilting pastures shake
the web of silence, but your look
seldom travels from your book.
The sun takes a turn round the lake.

Only when evening throws the last
steamer like a dart burning past
the point, and ghostly waiters
whisper that supper is soon,
will you stumble down as the moon
stumbles on the tideless waters.

The moon is a periscope in which
an exile like myself may watch,
over mountains rough as broken glass,
others who prepare to make
their longest journey from the lake
into the formidable pass.

All see only the green incline.
So many have crossed that skyline
singing, and none of them come back
to tell how night in the ravine
cut them off like a guillotine,
still there is singing on the track.

Darkness and mist and the false echo
divide the singers, and snow
cancels each step. Some as they clamber
lonely over glaciers find,
imprisoned under ice, a friend
like an insect in green amber.

But here the sun, in rising, makes
bonfires of the embattled peaks.
Winds have sung with us; and we
in exultation have seen,
distant but luminous between
mountain and mountain, the tidal sea.

Little sisters, about to climb
beyond your valley for the first time,
what can I give you – talisman
or map – that may guide you straight
into a plain as temperate
as the valley where we began?

Not my example, certainly.
Only my love – and this: I see,
whenever the going is rough,
those who defy foul weather
and avalanche are roped together
and the rope is love.

From W.B. Yeats to his friend Maud Gonne

From W.B. Yeats to his friend Maud Gonne.
The writing modest as the words upon
the title-page. Him I can understand;
picture him turning the pen in his hand
considering what to write: something not cold
nor yet embarrassingly overbold.
But in the gallery where my portraits are
I cannot see the heart that, set ajar
for anarchists and peasants and sick birds,
could not be crowbarred open by such words
as break the heart of time; that fountained out
in tears or laughter at a newsboy's shout –
only to the poet remaining shut
as these clenched pages that she never cut.

Toulouse Lautrec at the Moulin Rouge

'Cognac – more cognac for Monsieur Lautrec –
more cognac for the little gentleman,
monster or clown of the Moulin – quick –
his glass is falling! more!'
                              The Can-Can
chorus with their jet net stockings
and their red heads rocking
have brought the patrons flocking to the floor –
pince-nez, glancing down from legs advancing
to five fingers dancing
over a menu-card, scorn and adore
prostitutes and skinny flirts
who crossing arms and tossing skirts
high-kick – a quick
eye captures all before they fall –
quick lines, thick lines
trace the huge ache under rouge.

'Cognac – more cognac!' Only the slop
of a charwoman pushing her bucket and mop,
and the rattle of chairs on a table top.
The glass can fall no further. Time to stop
the charcoal's passionate waltzing with the hand.
Time to take up the hat, drag out the sticks,
and very slowly, like a hurt crab, stand:
with one wry bow to the vanished band,
launch out with short steps harder than high kicks
along the unspeakable inches of the street.
His flesh was his misfortune: but the feet
of those whose flesh was all their fortune, beat
softly as the grey rain falling
through his brain recalling
Marie, Annette, Jean-Claude, and Marguerite.

The Assault

As the mad woman cried out in the square,
when every hand was hauling on a rope
or levering gates from hinges there –
gates never forced in ten years' war:
'A rape is avenged, avenged with a rape!'

Because, being mad, she could not comprehend
the soldiers' back-slapping and the women's joy,
they did not stop her mouth or send
her packing as they strained
to manoeuvre the stallion into Troy.

The foreign god was of such size, the gate
so stiff, so narrow the ways of the town,
that though the heroes pulled their weight
and the crowd levered, it was late
before they threw their ropes and levers down.

As for a carnival or wedding rite
from every bracket in every room
pine torches fountained their scented light.
There had not been such a lovers' night
not since Paris brought that Helen home.

Embraced and garlanded, the soldiers all
with a girl on one arm instead of a shield
danced round the horse and round the wall
swallowing wine by the helmet full;
then two by two into the darkness reeled.

Only the mad woman huddled alone
in a doorway after, saw shadows fall
from horse's belly to pavement stone
and scatter, scatter, like leaves blown
into a shadow drift under the wall.

As the swan, as Paris, so now the horse
in the dark of the city dropped his seed.
Now life and death must run their course.
Foundations riven by that force
recoil already and the housetops bleed.

Mad woman, mad woman, mad woman – no –
feeling the city shudder, hearing it moan –
not mad enough – better to go
mad as the moon herself than know
the city's end an image of my own.

The Trap

The first night that the monster lurched
out of the forest on all fours,
he saw its shadow in his dream
circle the house, as though it searched
for one it loved or hated. Claws
on gravel and a rabbit's scream
ripped the fabric of his dream.

Waking between dark and dawn
and sodden sheets, his reason quelled
the shadow and the nightmare sound.
The second night it crossed the lawn
a brute voice in the darkness yelled.
He struggled up, woke raving, found
his wall-flowers trampled to the ground.

When rook wings beckoned the shadows back
he took his rifle down, and stood
all night against the leaded glass.
The moon ticked round. He saw the black
elm-skeletons in the doomsday wood,
the sailing and the failing stars
and red coals dropping between bars.

The third night such a putrid breath
fouled, flared his nostrils, that he turned,
turned, but could not lift, his head.
A coverlet as thick as death
oppressed him; he crawled out; discerned
across the door his watchdog, dead.
'Build a trap', the neighbours said.

All that day he built his trap
with metal jaws and a spring as thick
as the neck of a man. One touch
triggered the hanging teeth: jump, snap,
and lightning guillotined the stick
thrust in its throat. With gun and torch
he set his engine in the porch.

The fourth night in their beds appalled
his neighbours heard the hunting roar
mount, mount to an exultant shriek.
At daybreak timidly they called
his name, climbed through the splintered door,
and found him sprawling in the wreck,
naked, with a severed neck.

Sindhi Woman

Barefoot through the bazaar,
and with the same undulant grace
as the cloth blown back from her face,
she glides with a stone jar
high on her head
and not a ripple in her tread.

Watching her cross erect
stones, garbage, excrement, and crumbs
of glass in the Karachi slums,
I, with my stoop, reflect
they stand most straight
who learn to walk beneath a weight.

Camel

Though come down in the world to pulling a cart
piled high as a house-top, camel, your gait
proclaims, proclaims, proclaims the aristocrat.

Though your knees, like a clown's, wear bells that clash
whenever your cushion-feet cuff the street,
a greater clown behind you swings the lash

over your backside. History and he
are unacquainted. From your ancestors
you have inherited history;

philosophy becomes you like your hump;
nobility speaks louder than these sores
and bells and the sweat on your angular rump.

I have seen your nostrils flare to a wind
born nowhere in the port or festering slums,
but in the wastes beyond the wastes of Sind.

Heavily falls the lash. You neither turn
nor flinch, but hooded in your eyes there comes
a glint of snows above Baluchistan.

In the Street of the Fruit Stalls

Wicks balance flame, a dark dew falls
in the street of the fruit stalls.
Melon, guava, mandarin,
pyramid-piled like cannon balls,
glow red-hot, gold-hot, from within.

Dark children with a coin to spend
enter the lantern's orbit; find
melon, guava, mandarin –
the moon compacted to a rind,
the sun in a pitted skin.

They take it, break it open, let
a gold or silver fountain wet
mouth, fingers, cheek, nose, chin:
radiant as lanterns they forget
the dark street I am standing in.

The Face

On the wall above the basins in the barber's shop
a bland face, shaven like a full moon,
salutes the lathered citizen when he looks up.

In the cinema foyer, café and saloon,
at the orphan's shoulder and the widow's side,
floats a face convivial as a child's balloon.

Day after day, milk-churn teeth in a mouth as wide
as a newspaper column or a newsreel screen
welcome an ambassador, dazzle a girl-guide.

Blessed and benevolent full-face! But profile seen
framed in the window of a car, perhaps,
(unflagged and without escort, arrowing between

office and home), the contours of the mask collapse
and tighten. Fat smiles starve as thin as glass;
only to trespass on the frontier of the lips

should tyres, like tongues, spit on you as they pass.

First of the Migrants

First of the migrants, overnight they say
Naz flew to London. She will glide no more
vivid as a rainbow through this door
with her sketch-book under an arm. Today,
missing her small step, one imagines
the rainbow sari in a Georgian square
painting the wind; bus-queues turning to stare
at a bird of Paradise among pigeons.

Last Post

The Garden Member with the walking stick
grasped like a baton in his British hand
deploys his seeds against the spring attack.
Here thin red line and hollow square stand
stiff in his eye already: wind shot
and the sun's crossfire rake them but break them not.

He sites a trench, waves up more gardeners
to dig the front line in – 'This privet hedge
will give them cover but wants cutting'. Shears
scissor behind him. Idler on the edge
of the battlefield, lolled in a wicker chair,
I lay my book down, sniff the smokeless air,

and reflect that evening best becomes
the Imperial-Barrack style. Bearers now throw
tall shutters open on to empty rooms,
as men besieged prop corpses in a row,
gunner by rifleman each at his post
drawing the sniper's fire. Almost

I am deceived. Time, liquid now as light,
drains from the roofs and like a school of whales
the Club buildings surface into night.
Behind these windows and behind these walls
field-officers are pulling on their boots
and monkey-jackets, lighting up cheroots.

Rowels chime on the stair. Glasses chime after
down colonnades where civil servants talk
of civil servants and a fist of laughter
thumps the air. Some, shadow by shadow, walk
about the garden. At their coming, palms
like supplicants make their salaams.

Kites crowd in the peepul tree. The sun,
ripest of windfalls, plummets to the ground.
Time passes. Dinner gong like evening gun
recalls the Garden Member, and its sound
recalls my ghosts to their element. I
go in. From the top of the stairs the sky

has doubled its girth, the garden decreased
to a moat. The eye swims over and sees
ghost-minarets and shadow gables. East
and west of my window two embassies
island the dark with light – our Scylla
and Charybdis, Russia, America.

Around them and beyond them like camp fires burn
the town and harbour galaxies. Tonight,
how many sahibs, whiskey-fisted, turn
to the garden wall that bounds their sight;
sensing, uneasily, in the street
a menace abroad they cannot meet

with crossed Lee Enfields from the library wall?
Not many now: most are laid underground,
but armchairs like Titan bones lumber the hall,
humbling us. We are hushed by the sound
of their silence. Light but no voices come
out of their hundred windows. Watching them,

I am reminded of Heorot, home
of the good Hrothgar, in that season
when his bachelors' mouths were stuffed with loam
instead of boasts, laughter or venison –
Heorot with its high seat empty in the hall
and Grendel's shadow growing on the wall.

The Swimming Pool

The swimming pool by night in summer
lying floodlit, grape-green, from below,
holds up to us in its long mirror
beauty and indolence; but now –
struck by the lash of a late swimmer –

writhes with a hundred hands. This tender moon
bares knuckles, coolie knuckles, taut
as wire on pick and spade, in May's noon
furnace digging for the sport
of manicured hands in the monsoon.

The swimmer, turning with an otter swirl
in the deep end, revives the quick
convulsion of a sun-struck fool
of a navvy who broke his neck;
but that was soon smoothed over, as now the pool.

Tent-Pegging at Night

The four greys fidget as a torch-boy runs
down wind across the *maidan* lighting pegs.
Spurred now by trumpets they take off like swans
with steady necks above a blur of legs.

Headlong horsemen, when the flames blow back,
see them as flags over Panipat plain.
Louder than hooves and trumpets they invoke
the Most High God. Moghuls again

lean from the saddle. Beside the stirrup
their level lances stoop towards the mark –
stoop lower – kick – and catherinewheeling up
proffer their flames to the devouring dark.

'Here comes Sir George'

The boys wink at the boys: 'Here comes Sir George.'
Yes, here he comes, punctual as nine o'clock
with bad jokes buzzing at his ramrod back –
'Victoria's Uncle', 'Rearguard of the Raj'.

They do not know or, if they know, forget
the old fool held a province down larger
than England; not as a Maharaja
prodigal with silver and bayonet;

but with cool sense, authority and charm
that still attend him, crossing a room
with the *Odes of Horace* under his arm
and in his button-hole a fresh-cut bloom.

Honour the rearguard, you half-men, for it
was, in retreat, the post of honour. He –
last of the titans – is worth your study.
You are not worth the unsheathing of his wit.

The Peshawar Vale Hunt

The Peshawar Vale Hunt has gone to ground.
Over its earth foxes laugh
last, for the loud-mouthed master, horn and hound
are at a loss for sound.

In the Horseshoe Bar of the Club with half
an hour to kill, I raise my drink
in mock salute to a damp-mottled, buff
Hunt Breakfast photograph

of nineteen-ten. In coats of Kipling-pink,
the colour of their map, the bloody
subalterns and iron maidens link
arms, leer, try not to blink

before the camera blinks. If they could see
themselves now, grouped on the grass
in their insolent poses! History
has put down the mighty

from their family seats; tumbled them, arse
over crop, out of the saddle.
The poor inherit the earth; the middle class
take care of the brass.

You, with your hair parted down the middle,
officer, gentleman and all
that, today you are sentenced by little
brown men of less rare metal.

Empire Builder, with your back to the wall,
have you any last word to say?
'It is better to ride fiercely, and fall,
than never to ride at all.'

Cowboys

panther-footed saunter in the street,
who spinning six blunt sounds in the mouth's chamber
tongue-hammer them one by one when they meet.

Evening. Eyes sharpen under sombre
brims, drilling the distance for a spurt of hooves.
These wait only for the Stage to lumber

between sights, to squander their nine lives
(in a town now dead from the waist up,
for where are the children and the shopping wives?)

They saunter with slack hands, but at the drop
of a card will conjure guns out of thick air –
explode every bottle on the bar-top –

eclipse the lamp with a shooting star –
struggle under tables, until the one
with the grin knock senseless the one with the scar.

Justice done and seen to be done,
a bullet in front for one in the back,
the honest stranger on the white stallion

canters off singing. Shopkeeper and clerk
lunge to their panther feet in the one-and-nines,
saunter slack-handed into the dark,

and manfully ride home their bucking trains:
each wearing, like a medal, his chosen wound
to cancel the reproach of varicose veins.

Bread and Circuses

He went to the cinema; saw
an arena, faces, sand;
in either wall a door
opening, opening, and
in either door, a gladiator.

The toga'd emperor he saw stand
conducting his applause
with an outflung hand,
and the gladiators
looking up at him from the sand:

a classic frieze. Then a ring rain-
bowed down and metal struck
metal, flashed, struck again.
Feet circled in a ruck
of sand, scarred with a widening stain.

The candid camera rolled its eye
up to the Roman crowd;
hands hammering the sky,
wolf-throats baying aloud
that one of their own kind should die.

Cheated of action in that pause,
having no interest
in the white of eyes and jaws,
he looked down, half noticed
hands fastened on his knees, like claws.

Quiet Wedding

Waiting so patiently for Mr Right
the six-foot millionaire to carry her off,
she sat indoors and knitted. Every night
she supped and sipped a magazine; until
sitting too long by windows brought a cough;
the cough – too long neglected – brought a chill;
the chill brought on pneumonia. Her light
at lunchtime brought the caretaker. She died
with cases packed, her passport up to date.
Black car, white flowers arrived: a nephew cried
at the reception. From that afternoon
she smiled. Retiring early she slept late
fulfilling all her dreams of honeymoon,
virgin forever and forever bride.

Witch's Sacrament

'Ritual' is perhaps too large a word:
but every night the small-boned lady,
like a faggot of firewood, makes her eddy
against the solid men flooding homeward
over the bombsite to the Underground.
Her back to the dark tide, crouching, she unwraps
fish-heads (with paper eyes) and liver scraps.
Her familiars rise to meet her with no sound.

Through the fence's broken teeth they take
the witch's sacrament, and their eyes connect
with a flight of sparks, which suddenly break
formation and burn out. Returning under
the earth her step is supple, her eyes reflect
a bonfire flowering from the breast's tinder.

Feet off the Ground

On the ground floor the wealthy and their cats
minded each other's business, but above
in the topmost branches of the flats
two, like their neighbours, lived on crusts and love.

Sparrow jazz shook them awake; pigeon hymns,
sacred on Sunday, all the week profane,
composed at nightfall their haphazard limbs.
And a crow made its pulpit in the drain.

If sometimes, towards evening, he let fall
out of his fingers' nest a clutch of words,
singing poured out of the window, and all
her birds were poems and all his poems birds.

Green Thought

I do not know much about love, but I know
it is common as grass which, although
it refuse at times to take root on a lawn,
can bury a bombsite, split asphalt, and grow
in any ditch, niche, or gutter where winds blow
or sparrow-boys brawl. This much I learn
from an old man who has limped up the path
to warm his feet, and more than his feet, at our hearth.

His scrupulous tweeds and courtesy
have taken their place at the ritual tea
on Sunday afternoons; a ritual
for him, whose shrine this is, especially.
A girl, not yet his wife, runs for more tea
into the singing kitchen. From the hall
her footsteps chatter, and soon her face
will laugh in the mirror over the mantelpiece.

He is watching – over his cup between
fireplace and door – a princess not nineteen.
We too remember her, though she appears
to us as the tall, gaunt, tragedy-queen
whom illness kept indoors, who dressed in green
throughout all seasons. We remember tears;
agonies the doctors could not understand;
tantrums, and the last tantrum ended by her hand.

But most the legend of her funeral
dominates memory: how there fell,
miraculous as manna, a swift wing
of snow, not heavily like a pall
but thin as moonlight. It transfigured all
mourners to alabaster, cancelling
veils, toecaps, collars, cancelling the sound
of the white coffin lowered into the white ground.

Today as he talks, smiles, drinks his tea,
smiles, talks of earlier Sundays, I can see
one picture only: him, brought to the brink
of the grave, and the grave suddenly
healed with fine snow, and every tree
in sight bowing a moonlit head. I think
love is like that: merciful as snow
bandaging the bruised earth, white making the green grow.

ROOT AND BRANCH
(1969)

For Margaret and Geoffrey Keynes

and a house of more books than bricks
one book more. Not one to stand
with the gold-shouldered folio spines
of your first friends, the Donnes and Brookes
that fifteen years ago shook a boy's hand.

On how many Friday nights since then
has your front door sheared from my back
the shadow of London. Shadows
are smaller here: as of a pen
across a page, or branches black
on a lawn, lengthening as the light goes.

Last again of the village lights
this lamp in whose blond tent we talk
of the blackberry crop; of your
new Palmer; of my new playwrights
and poets; of an oak's cracked fork –
to be felled tomorrow with the re-set saw.

Grandchildren, come for Sunday lunch,
find us in the garden. They will learn
why all your trees bear fruit, perceive
the root's relation to the branch;
as I have done, who in return
bring you my thin crop hidden among leaves.

A True Confession
'Truth's a dog must to kennel'

The truth, the whole truth always
and nothing but the truth
ran like a tune through my schooldays,
a theme-song from the myth

of Gawayn and Galahad
and the high court of Arthur,
when Truth and Untruth, Good and Bad
wore different armour.

Truth as the order of the day
worked like a charm at first:
the boys that lied or ran away
always came off worst.

The primary abstractions
in conflict at that range
shivered their swords but broke no bones.
How soon perspectives change,

armour spits blood, true and untrue
look the one colour.
I learnt, after a clash or two,
truth was a killer

and killers must be locked away.
Locking him out of sight
has changed the order of the day
to the order of the night:

when into freedom tunnelling
through my sleep, the truth
breaks from its cell; incites the tongue
to mutiny in my mouth.

All night long the elaborate
armour of self-deceit –
forged so cunningly plate by plate –
falls bloodied at my feet.

Stepping at daybreak out of the lies
of friendship, lies of love,
expedient hypocrisies –
shield gone and visor, glove

struck off – here I unsheathe my pen,
resolved that if it miss
the truth I will begin again:
and lie even in this.

For poets are liars. Their lives
scan less than their smooth
confessions. But now and then our lies
betray us into truth.

The Postman

Satchel on hip
the postman goes
from doorstep to doorstep
and stooping sows

each letterbox
with seed. His right
hand all the morning makes
the same half circle. White

seed he scatters,
a fistful of
featureless letters
pregnant with ruin or love.

I watch him zig-
zag down the street
dipping his hand in that big
bag, sowing the cool, neat

envelopes which
make *twenty-one*
unaccountably rich,
twenty-two an orphan.

I cannot see
them but I know
others are watching. We
stoop in a row

(as he turns away),
straighten and stand
weighing and delaying
the future in one hand.

A rose is not a rose

in Our Gardening Correspondent's prose.

Crushed between SPIDERMAN'S ACCIDENT
and OSPREYS NESTING it gives off no scent

to sweeten our commuting breath.
On the walk from the station, with

yesterday's record crop of dead
and a column of births folded

under my arm, I enter
Smithfield where the porters saunter

among carcases. Snout by snout
pigs that the cleaver turned inside out

are hung, drawn, and quartered. Parts
I do not recognise loll from carts.

A solitary trotter
blanches as it stains the gutter –

making the eyes recoil, nerves shrink.

Blood is not blood when it is ink.

A Barbican Ash

City pigeons on the air
planing like surfers swirl in their
calm descent, skid on one wing
about a tree where no sapling
was yesterday. Their country cousins,
counties away, now circle in
search of a nest not to be found
between the holed sky and the holed ground.
Like a flag at its masthead frayed
with shot, in this I read
of a tree winched from a wood
to be set in a concrete glade.
Workmen today come packing
its roots with a chemical Spring.

Men are more mobile than trees:
but have, when transplanted to cities,
no mineral extract of manure,
hormone or vitamin to ensure
that their roots survive, carve through the stone
roots, cable roots, strangling my own.

Sensation

Yellow and poster-striped the hornet vans
swarm into view hymning Humanity,
Truth, and the Public Good – their glands
charged with the venom to infect a city.

Summer 1963

Telegrams

When the chrysalis broke
open in her hand
the white, hinged, wings
of the telegram shook,
as if to test the wind
of her altered breathing.

With a street in spate, torrents
of chromium between
my kerb and her doorstep,
I could not read the sentence
she unfolded when
her paper face looked up.

But a kind of love
extended my senses
beyond their frontiers.
I could hear above
the city insect voices –
locusts, jamming my ears

with their calls and the black-
lettered tide
of their wings. Telegrams!
Shortcircuiting the clock –
half the world in one stride –
they travel light as poems.

61

Heart stammer, hand stammer
printing the air;
the voltage of the nerve
discharged; but somewhere
answering, a tremor
unmistakable as love.

An Evening Walk

Taking my evening walk
where flats like liners ride
at anchor on a dark
phosphorus-rippled tide
of traffic, ebbing, flowing,
I heard from a kiosk
a telephone ringing;
from an empty kiosk.

Its dark voice welling up
out of the earth or air
for a moment made me stop,
listen, and consider
whether to break in
on its animal grief.
I could imagine
torrents of relief,

anger, explanation –
'Oh for God's sake' – but I'd
troubles of my own,
and passed on the other side.
All the same I wondered,
with every step I took,
what I would have heard
lifting it from the hook.

As I was returning
after the pubs were shut,
I found the bulb still burning
in the kiosk, but
the dark voice from the dark
had done with ringing:
the phone was off the hook
like a hanged man swinging.

As Others See Us

She finding on his lips
sour champagne, and he
on her hair confetti,
they enter that eclipse

the novels promise. She
in his eyes, he in hers,
melt as the moon devours
the sun. They do not see –

until a sixth raw sense
nags them to consciousness –
the eye against the glass
cold as a camera lens.

Sickened, they see in this
a creature double-backed
disturbed in a gross act.
The eye blinks, vanishes:

but still the staring pane
holds like a negative
her Adam and his Eve
unparadised again.

Harvest Moon

He at the sill saying
over again, *My God,*
will it ever stop growing? –
a question echoed
by the upturned faces
moonstruck in the road.

Weeks past her waning still
the moon grows. Pores become
pockmarks as her flanks fill,
filling the night sky. *Look,*
London would go under
if her waters broke.

Through porous curtains light
leaks, and through eyelashes
scalds the eye. Last night
she dreamt, as she fell
asleep, of a dark bird
breaking from a bright shell.

Two Hands

My father in his study sits up late,
a pencil nodding stiffly in the hand
that thirteen times between breakfast and
supper led a scalpel an intricate
dance. The phone has sobbed itself to sleep,
but he has articles to read. I curse
tonight, at the other end of the house,
this other hand whose indecisions keep
me cursing nightly; fingers with some style
on paper, elsewhere none. Who would have thought
hands so alike – spade palms, blunt fingers short
in the joint – would have no more in common? All

today, remembering the one, I have watched
the other save no one, serve no one, dance
with this pencil. Hand, you may have your chance
to stitch a life for fingers that have stitched
new life for many. Down the *Lancet* margin
his hand moves rapidly as mine moves slow.
A spasm shakes the phone at his elbow.
The pencil drops: he will be out again.

Thistles

Half grown before half seen,
like urchins in armour
double their size they stand
their ground boldly, their keen
swords out. But the farmer
ignores them. Not a hand

will he lift to cut them down:
they are not worth his switch
he says. Uncertain whom
they challenge, having grown
into their armour, each
breaks out a purple plume.

Under this image
of their warrior blood
they make a good death,
meeting the farmer's blade
squarely in their old age.
White then as winter breath

from every white head
a soul springs up. The wind
is charged with spirits: no –
not spirits of the dead
for these are living, will land
at our backs and go

to ground. Farmer and scythe
sing to each other. He
cannot see how roots writhe
underfoot, how the sons
of this fallen infantry
will separate our bones.

The Stone
After the Polish by Zbigniew Herbert

The stone
is a perfect creature

obedient to its own
bounds true to its nature

filled to its firm rind
with a stony meaning

with a scent to remind
no one of anything

to frighten nothing lure
nothing kindle no lust

its coldness and ardour
are dignified and just

I hold it guiltily
in my curved palm

its honourable body
dishonourably warm

stones cannot be tamed
looking at us will lie

to the end with undimmed
unwavering eye

False Alarm

After the Polish by Tymoteusz Karpowicz

The cry and the silence
after the cry turned out
the neighbours, ambulance,

policemen running: but
nobody's head, chest, arm
was bloody or bullet-

plugged. Finding the street calm
the crowd frayed at the fringe,
called it a false alarm –

as if only the tinge
of blood or bullet-singe
below the heart can be
marks of man's agony.

Firstborn

You turn to the window for the first time.
I am called to the cot
to see your focus shift,
take tendril-hold on a shaft
of sun, explore its dusty surface, climb
to an eye you cannot

meet. You have a sickness they cannot heal,
the doctors say: locked in
your body you will remain.
Well, I have been locked in mine.
We will tunnel each other out. You seal
the covenant with a grin.

In the days we have known one another,
my little mongol love,
I have learnt more from your lips
than you will from mine perhaps:
I have learnt that to live is to suffer,
to suffer is to live.

By Rule of Thumb

Leather and wood and stone –
meeting the grain of my thumb
with as rare a grain of their own –

ratify a treaty made
centuries back between
thumbprint and the print of hide,

the stubborn grain of flint
and the lithe grain of wood.
I track my thumbprint

through its coils. The lifeline
swerving hand over hand
goes to ground in one

clenched on an adze. Roughness
of shaft, blade, thong;
lines travelling to this

glove, pebble, tabletop
I turn towards, turning
from heartache with the sap

shrunk in its severed grain.
So many sinews cut.
Glove and table contain

felled herds and forests, and
a chain-gang hundreds strong
moves when I move my hand.

Glove, paperweight, and table
cut from the running grain
are whole, are serviceable,

and teach me how to take
my soundings with a line
that holds though the heart break.

The Fall of a Sparrow

Who disinherits
the son we endowed in the womb?
If not the hand of chance
dicing with chromosomes,
what strategy of Providence
cost our sparrow his five wits?

The comforters
speak of our windfall as the price
of a poet's licence –
the necessary sacrifice,
a pound of flesh no distance
from the heart. But the heart answers

no. Is a life
in the shadow to be outweighed
by the moving shadow
of a life across a page?
Does Providence sell a sparrow
for a song? Husband and wife

ask one another
the answer they never get right
night after night. Question
and answer turn tail at first light.
A cot shakes, and the fallen sun
rises for father and mother.

At Take-Off

No longer when the lights flick on
No Smoking, Fasten your Seatbelts ·
that picture – fading as the floor tilts
upward – of the stiff tarpaulin
over me dividing darkness
from darkness, and no stars: instead,
the snapshot of an unscarred head
falling behind me, fatherless.

On the Road

The red lights running my way
keep their distance, hold their fire; the white
blaze from both barrels as they
lunge past. Headlamp and tail-light

switch in the mirror, white to red,
red to white as gears shift down
to overtake. Shot through the head
with lights I sway from town to town.

Red corpuscles, white corpuscles,
thread the branched arteries.
Cramp gnaws my anklebone, worries
the calf-muscle

wired to a pedal. Untuned now
the athlete's pulse stumbles through fat
that once ran steady as the flow
of petrol under my foot.

Cylinders leaping at the swerve
of the road inherit
our animal blood; I hear it
answer the summoning nerve

in other arteries. I have been
how many years on the road?
The dashboard reels off a ribbon
of figures I cannot read

for the ricochet of lights
from windscreen and wet street.
Long enough to remember nights
when blood through all its channels beat

with one current marrying white
and red. The sky over London
burns like my forehead; heat without
energy, light without vision.

Bacillae spawn in the bloodstream,
but the stream has outrun its poisons
before. I thread a fever-dream
of crossroads, straining to read the signs.

Epilogue to an Empire
1600-1900
an ode for Trafalgar Day

As I was crossing Trafalgar Square
whose but the Admiral's shadow hand
should tap my shoulder. At my ear:
'You Sir, stay-at-home citizen
poet, here's more use for your pen
than picking scabs. Tell them in England
this: when first I stuck my head in the air,

'winched from a cockpit's tar and blood
to my crow's nest over London, I
looked down on a singular crowd
moving with the confident swell
of the sea. As it rose and fell
every pulse in the estuary
carried them quayward, carried them seaward.

'Box-wallah, missionary, clerk,
lancer, planter, I saw them all
linked like the waves on the waves embark.
Their eyes looked out – as yours look in –
to harbour names on the cabin-
trunks carrying topees to Bengal,
maxims or gospels to lighten a dark

'continent. Blatant as the flag
they went out under were the bright
abstractions nailed to every mast.
Sharpshooters since have riddled most
and buried an empire in their rags –
scrivener, do you dare to write
a little "e" in the epilogue

'to an empire that spread its wings
wider than Rome? They are folded,
you say, with the maps and flags; awnings
and verandahs overrun
by impis of the ant; sun-
downers sunk, and the planters' blood
turned tea or siphoned into rubber saplings.

'My one eye reports that their roads
remain, their laws, their language
seeding all winds. They were no gods
from harnessed clouds, as the islanders
thought them, nor were they monsters
but men, as you stooped over your page
and you and you and these wind-driven crowds

'are and are not. For you have lost
their rhythm, the pulse of the sea
in their salt blood. Your heart has missed
the beat of centuries, its channels
silted to their source. The muscles
of the will stricken by distrophy
dishonour those that bareback rode the crest

'of untamed seas. Acknowledge
their energy. If you condemn
their violence in a violent age
speak of their courage. Mock their pride
when, having built as well, in as wide
a compass, you have none. Tell them
in England this.'
                    And a pigeon sealed the page.

Kathmandu–Kodari

They are building a road out of Kathmandu –
sixty-three miles to be cut with the spade
and five tall bridges to be made
with baskets of cement and bamboo

scaffolding. They are building a road
to Kodari, a high road to be met
with ceremony in Tibet
by the Chungking-Lhasa-Kodari road.

What will they carry, these five tall bridges?
Coolies trudging northward under bales of rice
or troop-filled lorries
travelling south? Periwigged like judges

the Himalayas watch the road-gangs labour.
Today, though the road-gangs seldom look up,
Kangchenjunga wears a black cap:
and the wind from Tibet sweeps like a sabre.

A Prayer to the Virgin
*The Russian Orthodox Greek Catholic Church
of America, which is hoping to buy the icon
The Virgin of Kazan from an Englishwoman for
£178,500, is satisfied that the icon . . . is the
original one from Moscow cathedral.*
          The Times 19 November 1963

A refugee finds refuge: San
Francisco takes you in
despite the colour of your skin
and your place of origin,
Black Virgin of Kazan.

When waves over Europe ran
hill-high you crossed them without harm,
your jewelled son upon your arm.
Others were swallowed by the storm,
Black Virgin of Kazan.

Miracle-worker, citizen
of East and West, may those that do
you honour see in you
the mothers that have not come through
miraculously from Kazan.

A greater miracle would be done
if all your diamonds melted
into tears, if all your rubies bled;
and children, everywhere, had bread,
Black Virgin of Kazan.

War Song of the Embattled Finns
   1939

Snow inexhaustibly
falling on snow! Those whom
we fight are so many,
Finland so small,
where shall we ever find room
to bury them all?

Sword Music

All that Anglo-Saxon jazz
of *brond on brynie* stuns the ear
attuned to higher frequencies.

But as you wield the words they welded
the great worm bleeds; nor can its venom
scald that sprung edge as it scalded

the smith and the giver of rings.
The consonants keep their balance,
dark shine of the raven's wings.

Byrhtwold over Byrhtnoth:
*'Hige sceal þe heardra, heorte þe cenre,
mod sceal þe mare, þe ure maegen lytlað.'*

Words so tempered, forged on the tongue
from loyalty, tenacity,
and pride, time can but sharpen. Wrung

from such obsolescent ores,
their words outlast their weapons
and may outlast ours.

'The will shall be harder, courage keener,
Spirit shall grow as our strength falls away.'
from 'The Battle of Maldon'

A Portrait of Robert Capa

Three eyes in the mirror
behind the bar (one of them shut
since five o'clock) burn and burn out
in time to the mortar

like a severed vein
ejaculating on the night
jet after rhythmic jet of light.
'How did it go?' The brain

unreels its images
frame by frame: holding to the flash
troops kneeling by a stream to wash
unfamiliar faces;

boots on a white road show
their teeth; a corporal on his back
plays with a puppy and a stick.
'Robert, what'll you do

when the war is over?'
The third eye lifted in a mute
rejoinder to the gun's salute,
blinks at the mirror

before the concussion
succeeds the flash. 'I cover
a war that will never
be lost, never be won.'

A poem about Poems About Vietnam

The spotlights had you covered [*thunder*
in the wings]. In the combat zones
and in the Circle, darkness. Under
the muzzles of the microphones
you opened fire, and a phalanx
of loudspeakers shook on the wall;
but all your cartridges were blanks
when you were at the Albert Hall.

Lord George Byron cared for Greece,
Auden and Cornford cared for Spain,
confronted bullets and disease
to make their poems' meaning plain;
but you – by what right did you wear
suffering like a service medal,
numbing the nerve that they laid bare,
when you were at the Albert Hall?

The poets of another time –
Owen with a rifle-butt
between his paper and the slime,
Donne quitting Her pillow to cut
a quill – knew that in love and war
dispatches from the front are all.
We believe them, they were there,
when you were at the Albert Hall.

Poet, they whisper in their sleep
louder from underground than all
the mikes that hung upon your lips
when you were at the Albert Hall.

T.E.L.

*Speed is the second oldest animal craving
in our nature . . . Every natural man
cultivates the speed that appeals to him.
I have a motor-bike income.*

Leader of insurgents he knew too much
of sabotage – raids from within, raids from
behind – to hazard, even in the touch
of hands, an insurrection nearer home.

Heroes he knew from the good books mutiny
against themselves: and when his legs bestrid
the desert ocean, unlike Antony
he let no Cleopatra break his stride

and flaw the epic. After blood and ink
were dry, he still denied the oldest
animal craving. Engine and petrol-tank
pulsing beneath him were sweeter than breast

and thigh: and as boys from the barrack hut
bounced their women, nightly, over the hill
he straddled an ideal more passionate
and in its passion subject to his will.

Embracing, like Hippolytus, a wind
that kissed the lips back from his teeth, he came –
rarest of lovers – to the long-imagined
consummation equal to his dream.

A Word with The Baas
Cecil John Rhodes

Well, my colossus, how do things look
from your view of the world? Is it
only seventy years and a bit,
one man's lifetime, since you shook

your finger at the map and said –
your shadow darkening immense
mountain-cross-hatched continents –
'Africa, I want it red'?

One man's lifetime but many lives,
all tributaries, like your own
turbulent pulse, of that pulse grown
to a river whose dark volume drives

a continent. Africa feeds
off blood like a vampire bat
and is not filled, does not grow fat
though a redcoat regiment bleeds

on the assegai. She can digest
a million head of cattle, mobs,
impis, and you: and still the ribs
tentpole her skin, and still her breast

for all that blood yields only dust
and marketable stones. For these
the white tents swarmed over Kimberley's
kopje, sudden as a locust

plague. Gold reef and diamond,
magnetic under tons of earth,
swung the heads of your oxen north.
Beyond the Limpopo, beyond

the Zambezi, Sheba at noon
hung in a golden haze. The nights'
slow-marching glacier of lights
miraged the mines of Prester John.

But farm by *kraal*, as the Mafeking road
took you to its heart, the *Boy's Own* dream
of bullion ripened to a dream
of land. No frontiers furrowed

your mind's map – only the railway
trained on the north. Your skeleton key
to open Africa from sea
to sea ground in the lock. Today

in your Matopo eerie shut
forever at your own request,
are we to think you cursed or blessed
having a god's perspective but

impotence more than man's? No tongue
for thunder now, no thunderbolt
telegrams crossing the *veld*:
the market beared, concessions wrung

from stubborn *kraals*. All that is ended.
Felled or furled its Union Jacks,
Africa, many-coloured, mocks
your vision: 'Red, I want it red

from Cairo to the Cape,' you said.
Do your eyes ache for lids? Sharpeville,
Katanga, Ruanda, mingle
their streams. The river mounts. The red

river threatens its banks of flesh.
Pray that the gods, my colossus,
electing mercy, may be less
ironic than to grant your wish.

A Letter from Berlin

My dear,
                    Today a letter from Berlin
where snow – the first of '38 – flew in,
settled and shrivelled on the lamp last night,
broke moth wings mobbing the window. Light
woke me early, but the trams were late:
I had to run from the Brandenburg Gate
skidding, groaning like a tram, and sodden
to the knees. Von Neumann operates at 10
and would do if the sky fell in. They lock
his theatre doors on the stroke of the clock –
but today I was lucky: found a gap
in the gallery next to a chap
I knew just as the doors were closing. Last,
as expected, on Von Showmann's list
the new vaginal hysterectomy
that brought me to Berlin.
                              Delicately
he went to work, making from right to left
a semi-circular incision. Deft
dissection of the fascia. The blood-
blossoming arteries nipped in the bud.
Speculum, scissors, clamps – the uterus
cleanly delivered, the pouch of Douglas
stripped to the rectum, and the cavity
closed. Never have I seen such masterly
technique. 'And so little bleeding!' I said
half to myself, half to my neighbour.
                                    'Dead',
came his whisper. 'Dont be a fool'
I said, for still below us in the pool
of light the marvellous unhurried hands
were stitching, tying the double strands
of catgut, stitching, tying. It was like
a concert, watching those hands unlock
the music from their score. And at the end
one half expected him to turn and bend
stiffly towards us. Stiffly he walked out

and his audience shuffled after. But
finishing my notes in the gallery
I saw them uncover the patient: she
was dead.
        I met my neighbour in the street
waiting for the same tram, stamping his feet
on the pavement's broken snow, and said:
'I have to apologize. She was dead,
but how did you know?' Back came his voice
like a bullet ' – saw it last month, twice.'

Returning your letter to an envelope
yellower by years than when you sealed it up,
darkly the omens emerge. A ritual wound
yellow at the lip yawns in my hand;
a turbulent crater; a trench, filled
not with snow only, east of Buchenwald.

Elm End

I
Those cherubs on the gate
emasculated by the village boys
are now sole heirs to the estate.

The elms in the avenue,
planted through centuries
one for a daughter, two

for a son, within the year
will carry the timber-
merchant's mark. He walks here

sometimes on Sunday. The rings
on their trunks are numbered:
and a rip-saw sings

in his head seeing columns
of figures march and countermarch.
This Sunday comes

the snow, keeping him indoors:
but it re-vaults the avenue
and for today restores

that manhood the cherubs knew
when a lodge-keeper swung the gate
letting the phaetons through.

II
Don't worry the bell in the porch.
If its tongue is not tied
with rust, it will search

out a ghost from the scullery.
The handle demands both hands:
go in, go up. He will be

pillow-bound in the great bed
under the griffin's eye
that saw his father born, and dead,

and him conceived. His grandmother's
grandmother caged that bird
in its crest, stitching feathers

by candlelight for Charlie
riding to Waterloo.
Under her canopy

the griffin sees not the hollow
trunk, tackled by gravity, but
how far the roots stretch under snow.

III

The fires have fallen. He has drawn
the white acres up to his chin:
fingers grapple the lawn

that once they crawled on. Letting go
can be harder than holding on
or taking hold – as elms ago

the griffin's claw took hold
of these white acres. Letting go
is a language he's too old

to learn. The griffin grips
a scroll inscribed *Hold Fast*
between its talon tips.

Tonight or tomorrow
or tomorrow night
he will cease to echo

the wind in the chimney. Blinds
will be lowered. The snow
will cover his hands.

If then the bulldozer roars
at its kill, he will not hear,
nor see the road-gang's griffin flex its claws.

Old Flames

October, and I learn
from calendars and trees
to be my age – shed, burn
the scented memories

of summer. Too many
summers weighing me down
with unshed letters She
or She sent me, still done

up in ribbon. Ribbon,
permit me. Do you blush
to recall some permission
granted these fingers? 'Hush',

you whisper, letting slip
a blue-veined load
I lifted to my lip
at seventeen. Aloud

I try out her name: *Ann* –
who brought me to my senses –
first shall be first. Come, fan
my flame with your sentences

not for the first time, but
the last! And now, in order
of appearance, each lot
of letters grows a black border.

Angela, Jacqueline,
Astrid, go through the fire
for me. Their smoke gets in
my eyes as they mount the pyre.

The face in each photograph,
aged in a flash, caves in;
the perfect cheekbones slough
the perfect skin.

Who's that behind her? Ouch!
I burnt my fingers, but
never this much!
I can't put myself out!

Oh no! The letters She
sent back shrivel to hot
air! Our ashes mingle; She
loves me, She loves me not.

Hazel, I burn for you!
My life goes up in flames,
a kiss to end and outdo
all . . .
            The shapes of your names

melt in my mouth. Freelance
no longer I take my leave
of you with this last dance.
If you carry my love

in your personal luggage,
more than your ears will burn.
My phoenixes, act your age;
blaze and be reborn.

HAND IN HAND
(1974)

A Bottle of Ink

a black thread
reaching from here
to God knows where,
a thread to be broken
every black inch
of its blind way
into the labyrinth.
Tonight I have written
letters that say

I *love you* and
These days my
poems die
under my hand . . .

Signing my name
I wonder what
sentences lie
coiled in that squat
bottle from which those came,
and why we pay
out lines like this
knowing there is
no going back.

Elegy for a Mis-spent Youth

Now that the chestnut candles burn
for your birthday, thickening the air
with vapoured sap, my thoughts return
to the attic over the square,
the table with its open book
and a bottle in which the red
sun set, your dress over the back

of a chair, and the bed
where, nightly, drowsy with the fair
exchange of love and with the smell
of chestnut wicks lighting the square,
we never lay and never shall.

Words on a Paper Tablecloth

Tonight, seen through plate-glass
in a café beside the Seine,
the street is a water-colour.
Under the brush of the rain
umbrella after umbrella
grows to full size. They pass

and diminish, half moons,
through all the phases of eclipse
into a streetlamp's nimbus. There
one stops while lovers join lips,
regardless of the street's bright stare.
The rain is strumming tunes

on the sky they stand
under, a star whose horizon
sings. Their music seals them as tight
as our silence when they move on . . .
into the dark . . . into the light . . .
into the dark beyond . . .

Walking against the Wind

'Roast chestnuts, a shilling
a bag.' Shilling and bag
change hands by brazier light.
And there they stand shelling
plump kernels to plug
each other's mouth as tight

as with a kiss. She wears
his blue coat, but the wind
cannot touch him with that
hot nut in his hand
and her thawing fingers
moving towards his mouth.

They shelter in my mind
at midnight, as the brilliant
mosaic towers black out.
Walking against the wind
I wish them a blue coat
for coverlet; jubilant

knowledge of each other;
ignorance that it blows
nowhere on earth so cold
as nightly between those
whom God hath joined together
to have and not to hold.

Positives

1
Black window opposite
bright wall, a head and a lamp between,
a head as full of the night –
and no stars to be seen –
as the lamp is full of its light.

Through glass and a membrane
once painted with your miniature
the dark stares at the dark. The rain
spits at the glass. Is it dark with you,
dear face I may not see again?

All that we left unsaid,
undone, a swarm of bitter negatives,
tonight seethes in my head.
Nothing of our love lives –
the children you wanted

lie locked in my scrotum –
till I turn to the lamp-lit sheet,
and the pen stirs under my thumb
as your breast stirred under it,
and the words come.

2
Saying 'I love you'
and hearing 'I love you' spoken,
the last seal on the lips broken
by a foreign tongue,

I am not I; and who
are you; and why did our verb not
ever before mean this; and what
now is its meaning?

Dearest, if we knew
tonight more than the gods allow,
hearing their sentence, should we now
stand as we do?

3

They noticed together
how the mirror held them
as they held each other,
locked in an oval frame.

Such luminous lovers!
Was the light they floated in
lamplight, they asked each other,
or light beneath the skin?

And when they looked away,
leaving them for that night
wrapped in each other, they
glowed with a richer light.

In other rooms each tries,
through other nights, to piece
together widened eyes,
mouth, cheek, into a face

familiar as their own.
But darkness dissolves all –
except their mirror-icon
brilliant on the wall.

The patron saint of lovers – lips
still parted, their eyes bright!
Then each, though separate, sleeps
wrapped in remembered light.

4

Tonight is the night of the blue moon
for which we prayed
from midnight to high noon
so many nights and days.

It rises as we climb six flights
of stairs, radiant with such
voltage that stars and streetlights
blaze if our fingers touch.

The sky is a bell of blue metal
that finds its tongue when we lie down –
the room rocking a little
as the moon swings over the town.

One slow note from the sky's rim
flows into another. The heavens
open and we swim
through mounting seas of resonance –

crest after crest, and the seventh wave
foaming over all.
Blue moon, what a tide moves when you move!
What seabed shall contain it should it fall?

5

After the moth's kiss
and the bee's,
but not in a gondola, this
matched by no metaphor
but that reflection of itself,
the kiss that seals my groin to yours.

6

Why such drooping plumage
and so empty-throated
when I set you free?
And yet you lift your head
and sing and sing for me
when covered in her cage.

7

Waking, I caught the world off-balance,
I will not say off-true
for it has not righted since
my eyes opened to you

turning to me. To live
in our bodies till now
and never know them! We leave
a tilting bed knowing we know.

Love is yeast. My thoughts rise
level with God's, as high
white clouds remembering
you in a cornflower sky.

All roads this morning
run downhill, shining,
and I round every corner
with the sun in my eyes.

8

DISABLED SERVICEMAN
with a chestful of gongs
beating time on your mac
to the honky-tonk songs

your accordeon plays,
what made you turn and blaze
at me that song of all songs
today of all days?

My heart between your hands –
blown from its body –
contracts and expands
with the song she sung me,

which your accordeon,
transplanted, pumps through
my veins. Here's money, magician.
And a new song, love, for you.

After 'La Desserte'

Thank you, Matisse,
for the wide-hipped carafe
    you gave me this
    morning, half-

full of the red.
Ever since then it has
    blessed our bed
    with wine-dark light as

we lay loving.
And like pearl divers there
    sometimes coming
    up for air,

we drank a toast
of two or three to things
    lovers prize most –
    till evening brings

the question, how
can this carafe and heart
    be fuller now
    than at the start?

Pour Commencer

Take 1 green pepper and 2 tomatoes
and cut them into rings and hearts. Mix those
with olives, black olives, and go for a swim
in a green sea with her (or him).
Then serve your salad on two bellies. Pour
a little sun-warmed olive oil in your
salt navel, some vinegar in hers
(or his), and eat slowly with your fingers.
Empty the bottle. Open a second. Then
lick your plates. You will need them again.

So Much in Common

So much in common being not enough
we move on together, moving back
together down the shadowed tracks
that brought us, singly, under the one roof.

Under the sheet you take me by the hand
to meet a boy among the dunes
who calls you beautiful. I stand
in his footprints to kiss you, brushing the down

along your cheekbone with a salty tongue.
Help me to push the dinghy out.
She gybes again! You seize my coat
with my mother's hand when it was young

as yours, and capsized we jog together –
fingers stiff on the clinkered hull –
hour by numbing hour, until
trawlermen's hands haul us in, to slither

on a deck among mackerel. Slept that night
in a bristling blanket. Blinked
awake, dressed, knowing by instinct
that you too were dressing by mushroom light.

Our fingers meet on your father's landing,
tighten at the treacherous stair,
and we ride on a banister
into an orchard with its branches bending.

That log-stacked summerhouse at the wood's edge
stands on a frontier, where I stood
hearing a foreign language in my blood,
and swung an axe and hammered wedge

after wedge into oozing apple grain.
'How dark it is.' Give me your hand.
I'll tread the nettles down and bend
the brambles back. If we are lost again

we are lost together. But the dark is pricked
by a star, and the trees draw back
into shadowy rows as the track
turns to an avenue. We correct

our course by the star. And the star grows
to a planet, a window, a room
with a pressure lamp in full bloom
beside the bed. Breathless among pillows

we move on together. Our lungs
increase the flame till its bowl brims
over. The bed's alight, our limbs
blaze through the sheet! We have the gift of tongues,

speaking each other's language not with the mouth
only, but with bodies dumb
before. Now candid, they become
transfigured with the eloquence of truth.

The Source

*'The dead living in their memories
are, I am persuaded, the source
of all that we call instinct.'*
W.B. Yeats

Taking me into your body
you take me out of my own,
releasing an energy,
a spirit, not mine alone

but theirs locked in my cells.
One generation after
another, the blood rose and fell
that lifts us together.

Such ancient, undiminished
longings – my longing! Such
tenderness, such famished
desires! My fathers in search

of fulfilment storm through
my body, releasing now
loved women locked in you
and hungering to be found.

A Question of Form and Content

I owe you an apology,
love my love, for here you are
in a school anthology
without so much as a bra
between your satin self and those
who come upon us in crisp sheets.
What they will make of us, God knows,
but no harm's done if it's

101

what we make of each other. Let
them observe, love, our *enjambement*.
They shall be guests at the secret
wedding of form and content.

Daybreak with Horses

All I could hear when he stiffened and listened
was the break in our hearts' antiphonal drumming,
and I ached that his thoughts should be distant
from mine, until I heard the horses coming –

a cascade, an avalanche, as if daybreak
were audible, light crashing from the roofs.
We swung ourselves down and my ache
was drowned in the torrent of hooves.

He lifted the curtain and side by side,
naked, we watched them pass: the greys, the black,
bay mares and chestnut, with a groom astride
each burnished and curvetting back.

And when the curtain dropped on a still street
majestic presences surged through the room,
I heard my name and how my pulses beat
as I kept pace with them under my groom.

Breakfast in Bed

Lying in late:
two croissants, warm
in each other's arms,
on a dazzling plate.

Personal Column

A GOLD LOCKET lost in the street
sometime between heartbeat and heartbeat.
Hinge sealed with the salt from two bodies
whose likeness neither side now carries.
Reward offered: happiness such
as the locket saw from its niche
bless whoever returns it. But
whoever finds and will not part
with it, may the miniature last
night mirrored in his heart be lost
today and found in another heart.

A Pair of Gold Dolphins

At sundown, two dolphins
enter the molten bay . . .
and from some other shore
I have seen those gilded fins
stitching the sea before.

Not Curaçao, black
fins only in Tarquah Bay,
silver the hurdling schools
off Delos . . . At my back
the burning mountain cools.

Its shadow puts out to sea.
And I suddenly know
that if that racing stain
outstrips my memory
they will never surface again.

Too late, for the killer
fin strikes – but look, they leap clear –
imperishable! A pair
of gold dolphins glitter
in the waves of a woman's hair.

Message Received

They come together again,
the luminous swift hand over the slow,
and though the watch-pulse does not quicken
as mine quickens, I know

that in another country
a pulse is answering the morse of mine.
Link by link you turn your bracelet slowly,
transmitting the call-sign

of a charged heart. It comes,
clear as Orion tonight, above
the crickets shrilling in the gums.
Out of the darkness, love,

I have your message always
at this hour: in spirit tenderly,
as once tenderly otherwise,
you are receiving me.

African Violets

indigo skies
each with its own full moon
shadow the desk. My eyes
stray from my papers. Soon,
forgetting the flowerseller
and the work I meant to do,
I shall persuade myself
these came from you.

Homecoming

At 40,000 feet
the dulled blade glimmers as it goes in
steadily, peeling dark skin
from the world turning under it,

and you throw back bedclothes.
Dazzled, when the plane lands
we converge with our lives in our hands
and the peeled sky sweet in our mouths.

Picnic

Those daisies know too much!
Seeing that kiss, and now
touching what they touch
ought to have made them bow

their heads. You, pressing her thigh –
because you dared to look
your rival in the eye –
shall be pressed in a book.

The Play of Hands

'I am the capital', head says,
'and what I say goes
for the barbarous provinces,
fingers and toes –'

as, at the frontier, a thumb
enters the tender groove
between index finger and thumb;
and though your fingers move

with a moth's tact in my hand,
the fire they kindle vaults
from province into province
and the capital melts.

Willow-pattern Blues

The willows are gold again
that have been black that have been green,
and I am back where I have been
with the willow-pattern blues
on a juke-box brain.

Down where the willows comb
their hair and a bridge makes mouths in the stream
we walk in a willow-pattern dream;
at midday kicking off shoes
where the grass whispers welcome,

and an emerald thread
shuttles downstream and back. 'We should live
like the kingfishers, love,
and never lose
today's lustre', you said.

And still, however unwise
or unlucky we seem, the kingfisher weaves
between leaves and reflected leaves
in a world contracted to
your willow-pattern eyes.

Through a Glass

Mid-day, mid-summer
in the middle of England.
The sun on my shoulder,
a glass chill in my hand
lifting to touch lips
with your chill glass. 'To us.'
As the lager lens tips
your face into focus,
it shows you distant, blonde
as the willow behind
you, blonde as the barley
across the lager-bright
river. What can there be
for us but sunlight,
sunlight, sunlight beyond
the chill glass in my hand?

A Dinner of Herbs
with Natalia Volokhova

I

A man in his shirtsleeves,
in front of a window brushed
by restless, importunate leaves,

is translating words put to a stove
or a hissing lamp or the wall
by a man translating his love

into Russian syllables.
In the mouth of the shirtsleeved man
roll words as cold as pebbles

with no more life of their own
than moves in the mouth of the Russian
under his lettered stone . . .

II

You enter the room with a tray
and, when I savour the rich steam
rising from your casserole, say:

'A dinner of herbs where love is.'
I relearn at your hands,
as deftly they fill the dishes,

a lesson learnt long ago.
Sitting cross-legged on the floor
we talk of Shakhmatovo

until the lamp gives up its ghost.
Your head sinks to my shoulder.
And with leaves whitening into frost

against a trembling window,
we make love by stovelight
to the sound of snow.

The Last Word

Words, words, you and your damn
words! she said and went out
like a whirlwind, slam-
ming the door.

           I was about
to say: that without words,
my love, where should we be
today? And afterwards
stripped to our names and two
cold dates, where shall we be
but in these words for what
we touch and are and do?

In the Zoological Section

We stop in front of the case
containing skulls of two roe deer
who brought each other to this place.

Their antlers interlocked, they lie
eye-socket to eye-socket
as, starving, they lay eye to eye;

breath mingling as the hours pass,
eyes clouding over, like our own
reflected in the cabinet glass.

Again

I have been there again, and seen the backs
convulsing at the heart of the bazaar,
spasmed with laughter and the lunging jar
of shoulders as the fruit is thrown. A crack

in the crowd wall brought me to the ring
where, linked so one at first could not tell which
was which, the pie-dog and his trembling bitch
suffered the tribesmen's pitiless pelting.

Though terrible their straining from each other,
her crying and his scabbed flanks shaken
with hurt and terror – worse to waken
from that harsh sobbing to the bed's shudder.

The Beginning of the End

1
Passing the great plane tree in the square –
and noticing me noticing
the railing's sawn-off arrowhead
ingrown too many rings deep there
in 1940 to be shifted –
you ask me what I am thinking,
and wish the words unsaid.

2

'Our' café

> *since a morning*
> *not to be talked about*
> *these mornings*

            has put out

its tulip awning,
and the bell above the door
like a clockwork canary
sings its one song.

> *As we*
> *crossed this chequerboard floor*

'Buon giorno'

> *affable*
> *as if we were regulars.*
> *Setting down our saucers*
> *on the glass-topped table*

'Due grandi neri –
this morning, please,
you are my guests. The lease
finito. I shall be
with the vino rosso
next month in Tuscany.
No more grandi neri,
no more espresso.'

Spilt coffee

> *spelt my name*
> *and your name, linked, on this*
> *glass table – our knees kiss-*
> *ing under it.*

            The same

finger writes TUSCANY
and rubs it out. We have
run out of words

> like love.

Next month where shall we be?

3

Getting up to go.
'My gloves!' Floor, seat,
handbag – 'oh no, no,
not in the street!'

> *My first present. It*
> *seemed right and proper*
> *enough. 'A perfect fit'*
> *said the girl in the shop*
> *as one hand pushed*
> *the other, finger by*
> *finger, home; and you blushed*
> *to meet my eye.*

Stripped of their shadows,
disconsolate hands stare
at each other and those
inert elsewhere –
the warmth and scent
of their fingers failing,
trampled on the pavement,
impaled on a railing.

Making an End

We call them ours, the leaves we saw –
hand in hand on our daily walk –
bud and break out across the park.

> *If kisses were leaves, we*
> *could cover that tree.*

We could hang every twig – and more,
every twig in the avenue –
with a tear spilt since. But have to
do something else: the hardest thing.
After so much, sharing so much,

those ducks in their patch
of daffodils making
love, last year,

nothing is harder
than making an end.

Their love-talk
followed us on our walk

where today a man on a ladder
is cutting a branch from a tree.
His power-saw snarls as its teeth
take hold, and we underneath
can hear not a word but only
the snarl and the snarling echo.
This is the gate. We have to go
through.

Think how we entered
it first!

The man raises his saw
as if to acknowledge us or
waving goodbye (the unspeakable word).

There are no words. And there must be
no looking back. Ten paces, twenty.
Like duellists we turn. Your mouth seems
to be open, black. Your right hand
flutters. The saw screams.

Apollinaire Trepanned

remembers the red
poem hot from his head
in the palm of his hand.

As rubber gloves
lifted my lid
with my helmet, did
an uprush of doves

flutter the nurses? When
will the birds that filled
my green branches build
there again?

Burning the Stubble

Another harvest gathered in
worse than the last; only a bin
of rotten grain for all our trouble.
But there is a time for the plough,
a time for harvesting, and now
a time for burning the stubble.

Flames snap at the wind, and it
etches the eye with a bitter
mirage of summer. Returning
I looked for the dip in the ground,
the nest, the unfurled poppy; found
nothing but stubble burning

and charred ground hardening towards frost.
Fire before ice; and the ground must
be ploughed after burning the stubble,
the ground must be broken again.
There can be no new grain
without, first, burning the stubble.

In the Park

Hugging his dolphin, our stone boy stands
snared in his fountain's frozen bowl.
The trees overhead are holding hands

two by two to the avenue's ends;
the hand in my pocket worries a hole.
Hugging his dolphin, our stone boy stands

with eyes for nothing but his friend's
blunt head. Why should he care that, bole to bole,
the trees overhead are holding hands

when yours and mine are in different lands
and remembered fingers worry a hole
in my heart? Our stone boy stands

hugging his dolphin as night descends
slashing my face with a wind from the Pole.
The trees overhead are holding hands

and talking in low voices. Mine pretends
there's nothing to say but that, in his bowl,
hugging his dolphin our stone boy stands;
the trees overhead are holding hands.

Resurrection

At midday the tree
in the garden throws
a net over me.

Restrained by shadows
as if, while I lay
at its foot, roots rose

and closed over me,
I can feel only
the pulse of the tree.

It draws up, steady
as mercury
from my dark body,

columns of clear
sap. Distilled to this,
I could lie here

forever, putting
my heart into
building and rigging

a beech trunk to climb
every year at this
leafmaking time.

And every year
under me singing,
swinging, I should hear

children whose fathers
call to them nightly
moving among the stars.

The Writing on the Wall

Open the window, let in the wind
to the room where the stencilled crate
and trunks with our dead selves coffined
in them dark hour by dark hour wait
for morning and the carrier's men.
Give them a sailing wind, and let
it sweep out the bad dreams, broken
dreams, memories we would forget.

At midnight last night wind and moon
were up together, and the tall
acacia at the wind's dictation
scribbled in shadow on that wall
writing I couldn't read; then struck
it out and wrote again. I've been
awake since, trying to break
its code, but now the wall's wiped clean.

Throw all the windows open. Here
it comes, the breath of the dead
smelling of garlic and stale beer
and smoke. And blowing us good
or ill? I could almost believe
in a change of tune, a new note
this morning as we leave
for wherever, whatever the wind wrote.

Mother and Child

Lighter by a life, you settle back
into a dune of pillows;
remembering, as the tide runs slack,
its current the night it rose
wrestling through you, lifting inland
the unknown here, at the tide's return,
made known, breathing under your hand.

Black grapes, as long in the growing, torn
from shrunk capillaries of the vine,
bleed in your mouth, letting the rain
sucked by the sun from the raw earth
run back into the earth again.

At Bedtime

Reading you the story you cannot understand
any more than another, before the light
goes out, I am distracted by the hand
turning the page too early or too late –

as I was in the bookshop, hearing today
that other father with the small son say:
'We need a book. What would you recommend
for a four-year-old starting to read?'

And a dam in my head broke under the thought
of things your simple hand would never make:
toys, love, and poems scattering the comfort
of commandments you can never break.

The Almond Tree Revisited

He looks up, wondering why
we've stopped, to see a pink cloud cross
the untroubled blue of his eye.

And not knowing how it was
seven years back, he tugs me on.
When I was acquainted with loss

you blessed me with a vision
of blossom welling from dark veins.
Today, with my light-headed son,

I stand in your shadow again
troubled with loss: the loss of power,
not his, but mine, the poet's an-

cient power of giving praise and honour:
in gratitude, blessing a tree
above its kind with a continual flower.

This Morning

The weathercock once again heading south
catches the sun's eye, and my daughter says
the blackbird has a crocus in its mouth.

'Spring's here',
                    I tell her.
                                        'Here for always?'
'No, but for now.'
                              'Now is for always,
now is for always',
                              she sings, as she takes
my hand and we take each other to school.

'I'll pick you some flowers and I'll make you cakes
and I'll swing in the sun all afternoon.'

And I'll spend half the night with a worn pen
in that worn hand you're holding, one half-moon
eclipsed by a bruise, writing again
something I cannot say: that now is not
forever and to have is not to hold,
but they, you will learn, have nothing, that
have nothing to lose. Your fingers unfold
their first, delicate leaves. Among them, may
the bird in your hand set your veins singing
from moment to moment, always,
as mine do this morning.

A FAMILIAR TREE
(1978)

The movement of humanity, arising as it does from innumerable arbitrary human wills, is continuous.

To understand the laws of this continuous movement is the aim of history. . . .

The peasants say that a cold wind blows in late spring because the oaks are budding, and really every spring cold winds do blow when the oak is budding. But though I do not know what causes the cold winds to blow when the oak-buds unfold, I cannot agree with the peasants that the unfolding of the oak-buds is the cause of the cold wind, for the force of the wind is beyond the influence of the buds. I see only a coincidence of occurrences such as happens with all the phenomena of life. . . .

To study the laws of history we must completely change the subject of our observation, we must leave aside kings, minister, and generals, and study the common, infinitesimally small elements by which the masses are moved.

LEO TOLSTOY, *War and Peace*

At the Church of St John Baptist,
Preston Bissett
May 1974

Dear John, if a sinner may so
address a saint in his own house,
I come, as others about to go
on a journey have come to these
worn steps, through seven centuries,
to ask a blessing, make their vows,
and look for assent, a sign from your window.

Here they received the names that are
all that remain of them, brown ink
in a parish register,
a shadow on lichened stone:
and among those lifelines, my own.
It draws me outside to the brink
of their graves and it draws me further.

Let me go down to them and learn
what they learnt on their journeys.
And in the looted cavern
of the skull, let me restore
their sight, their broken speech, before
from these worn steps or steps like these
speechless to the speechless I return.

ENGLAND

Mother and Son
1738

Hush-a-bye baby   on the tree top
I am thy tree and thou
my acorn   an the Lord allow
shall grow to rock acorns and drop

them and see saplings grow in thy shade
Hush-a-bye baby   baby no more
Baby thou went in at the church door
and John thy father   when the parson laid

white hands on thee   said Let his name
be John   *And whatsoever*
Adam called every living creature
that was the name thereof   Thou came'st

hush-a-bye baby   baby no more
John from the font   into the sun
the churchyard where the sexton
was talking to the wind   Thy father bore

thee through the village like a prize calf
greeting the neighbours' God
ha'mercy with a grave nod
a nod for the shout across fields   the laugh

from a thatcher's ladder   So many years
at my goodman's side
stretching my stride
to keep step with the grazier's

and him still a stranger   When the wind blows
the cradle will rock   Sown
in me   grown in me   known
to me always   There   the cock crows

My dearest stranger stirs   and soon the bed
will grumble   shaken to its roots
as he swings out   groping for his boots
He has a calf too   lowing to be fed.

Old John Young John
1744

The day my father stayed in bed
Aunt said   Ann   send the boy out
but I said father said
he would teach me to tickle trout

Not today   nor any day
Aunt said   So I went out and scratched
the pig's back   gave the horses hay
and all the morning watched

them come and go   the other aunts
and neighbour women   all with their
aprons to their eyes   old Chance
the joiner   sniffing the air

and Mister Pearse with his Good Book
At midday mother called me in
Father was lying on his back
with a cloth tied under his chin

Today he came down   in a chest
the uncles carried   set down   let
down   *That which thou sowest*
is not quickened   except

it die   die   halfway to Hell
he stared from darkringed knots   I could
hear him   his hands   as the clods fell
on him   hammering the wood

I was lying above the place
where he caught the freckled trout
when there   far down   was his face
very white   and one hand stretched out

Before I could seize it with mine
the pike   struck   the water boiled

Hush   he is sleeping   Sleep thou   child
and wake a man   his four fields thine

To *the Honourable Members*
of the House of Commons
1782

Sirs:
      We the undersigned
Freeholders, Farmers, Cottagers
of Preston Bissett, being of one mind,
beg Leave to represent
that those Persons of this Parish
with immemorial Entitlement
to Common Right on Lands some wish
now to inclose, would be deprived thereby
of an inestimable Benefit.
The Beasts they graze on the said Lands supply
their Families with Milk and Meat
in the clenched Belly of the Year,
and furthermore, they now produce
lean Cattle for the Grazier
to fatten and bring at a fair Price
to Market. This we conceive to be
the shortest Path
to Public Plenty and Prosperity,
and we conceive the Aftermath
of the Bill before the House
to be Depopulation of a Village

now filled with vigorous
and hardy sons of the Tillage,
from whom, and the Inhabitants
of other open Parishes,
the Nation has supplied those Regiments
and Fleets that through the Ages
have been its Strength
and Glory. Driven from the Soil
into the swollen Towns, they must at length
be so enfeebled by their Toil
at Loom and Forge as to debilitate
their Posterity and thence
by slow Degrees obliterate
that Principle of Obedience
to the Laws of God and Man,
which forms the Character of such
as have the Right of Common,
and on which Principle so much
depends the Government
and good Order of the Realm.
These, the Petitioners represent,
will be the Injuries to them
and evil Consequences to the State
of the Inclosure now proposed,
as elsewhere it hath been of late,
and being thus exposed
they pray the House (the Constitutional
Protector of the Poor) to heed
this their Petition that the Bill
may not be suffered to proceed:
and have the Honour to remain
etcetera, Will Richardson,
Josiah Quainton, Henry Payne,
John Stallworthy, Will Orchard, Thomas Dunn.

In the Name of God Amen

Bowing and scraping   the notary's pen:

*This is the last will and testament
of*

whom had he the honour to address?

John Stallworthy

and my employment?

Grazier

of what parish?

*Pres-
ton Bissett in the county of Buckingham*

Name of God   name of grazier
name of parish   Where does a name
come from   what is it worth

*in the year
of our Lord one thousand eight hundred
and six*

What had I to bequeath?

*my soul into the hands of God
and my body to be laid beneath
a decent stone*

my goods and chattels?

*unto my wife Ann Stallworthy
Also my stock of cattle
and implements of husbandry
And I bequeath unto my sons
John Stallworthy and William
Stallworthy*

                    faith in God's mercy   none
          in the justice of men

                              the sum
     of twenty pounds apiece

                              my property?
          Less to my name in life
          than the churchyard holds for me

     It is my wish that my said wife
     Ann shall succeed me as occupier
     of the land I hold and occupy
     of Thomas Coke Esquire

          once open as the open sky

The Birds o' the Parish
   circa 1810

Spring come early, spring come late,
When the oak put on its leaves,
The martin and the swallow
Would build beneath the eaves.
But since the squire 'closed the common,
Men take the road to town
And thatch where nestlings grew and flew
The wind and rain pull down.

   Spring come early or late today,
   The birds o' the parish are vanisht away.

Summer come early, summer come late,
The pigeon and the rook
Would lease between the women
Behind the reaping hook.

But since the squire 'closed the common
And leasin's called a crime,
Men go to prison for it
And birds are snared in lime.

Summer come early or late today,
The birds o' the parish are vanisht away.

Autumn come early, autumn come late,
The ouzel on the briar
Would sing with those who hewed a log
To feed a cottage fire.
But since the squire 'closed the common
And cleared it for the plough,
The poor man must burn cattle dung –
Until he lose his cow.

Autumn come early or late today,
The birds o' the parish are vanisht away.

Winter come early, winter come late,
When icicles grew on the hedge
The sparrow never lacked a crumb
Left on a window ledge.
But since the squire 'closed the common,
The poor are starving so
The sparrow on the window ledge
Must stiffen in the snow.

Winter come early or late today,
The birds o' the parish are vanisht away.

William
1815

Bells   dinting the afternoon
from Buckingham   Gawcott   and then
the clappers of Bissett   bang   bang
as if Christ were risen again
on a Thursday in June

Happen a great fire   but no smoke
Legged it over the fields   bang   bang
the heart under my smock
to *Victory   Boney to hang*
from an English oak

Tankards passed from The Old Hat
a health to the Duke   one more
and a health to his men   bang   bang
Who dragged the cart out   wood   straw
and the pitch-barrel   who fired that

Tankard empty   tankard full
Brawling for a suck at the bung
Dark   where   what field   nettles my tongue
No quarter   cannon bells   bang   bang
break tower   sky   skull

To Samuel Greatheed, Evangelist, Newport Pagnell Chapel
1822

Good Master Greatheed,
                    do you mind
the boy at Preston Bissett where
you preeched by the In? I am he
lost without light. How do I find
the wickett gate? I pray you gyde
your servant, Sir,
                    George Stallworthy

News From Home
1831

My nephew,
                    Have our troubles come
to your godly ears? Red sky at night
a rick alight, and at Wycomb
last month the bloodiest fight
I ever saw. Came shouts at dawn,
uproar outside the inn, the sound
of feet and a rallying horn.
It was a band of labourers bound
on violent business, so their staves
and sledgehammers declared. One called
my name: he with the horn, Ned Graves,
your school-fellow. 'We're one and all!'
said he. I fell in step with him,
asking what brought him there. 'A purse
and belly with nothing in them.'
I prayed him keep the peace lest worse
befall. At which he blew his horn.
We had come to the edge of town
and a mill, whose gates were soon sawn
from their hinges. Someone threw down

vitriol and many were burned
as they burst in. The new machines
were sledgehammered till no cog turned
another. There were violent scenes
at other mills. A cleric read
the Riot Act. 'Be off and claim
your thirty pieces!' shouted Ned.
And then the soldiers came.
                    Today at Aylesbury I heard
false witness from a man of God.
God repay him. It went hard
with Ned. Transported – dreadful word –
for seven years. Because he had
no work, transported seven years.
Because his children cried for bread
at night, transported seven years.
Because he blew a horn, because
a vicar valued the truth less
than tithes, transported seven years.
How, if the shepherd so transgress,
shall sheep not stray? Are there not rams
caught in our thickets, and can you
not set them free? Are heathen lambs
more hungry than our own? Nephew,
your fathers' flocks are calling. Shall
they call in vain?
                    John Stallworthy

Patchwork
1833

A house without a man
a pod without a pea
William gone   under the ground
George going   over the sea
Come little needle   you
and I have work to do

133

Grey silk   for the village
William's wedding vest
and this for God's Acre
my cotton Sunday-best
with the Michaelmas daisies
He always liked these

For Claydon Brook   a ribbon
Lenborough Wood   sateen
remnants of chintz and twill
the crowded fields between
and from this pair of sleeves
a border of oak leaves

Though seas be heaped between us
my son shall sleep at home
and when he takes a bride
may she find here with him
on this familiar ground
what William and I found

The Tuscan
16 October 1833

My dear uncle,
                    Lying tonight
at Gravesend, joyful augury
of our journey's end, I write
from a full heart.
    As we came aboard,
a cloud inland outran the rest
unfurling, as it swirled toward
us, wings that darkened the bright West,
shadowed the shore and estuary.
Above the listening ship it broke
and every mast became a tree
again, budded with birds. They spoke

to me shrilly of home, their mud
nests under your eaves, and your voice
calling me. But the voice of God
was calling them South. I rejoice
to have heard His summons. May His cloud
of witnesses speak in the Spring
to you: of heathen fields well ploughed,
well planted and worth harvesting
as any in Preston Bissett.

 Although you cannot approve
or bless my choice, do not forget
one who remembers you with love,

   Your nephew George

THE MARQUESAS

PAGES FROM A JOURNAL

The Departure
17 October 1833

From Gravesend on the morning tide.
God forgive me that I wrote
'a joyful augury', in my pride
forgetting poor Ned Graves, afloat
in irons. On deck, thinking of him
between decks, watched the harbour sink
beneath our wake and sang a hymn
to mend my spirits.

The Arrival
22 March 1834

Only the wind was up before me
and the man at the wheel, who said,
'Listen, her timbers talk in their sleep,
the masts sing a new song. When she
smells land, you can give her her head.'
Darkness was upon the face of the deep.

The spirit of God moved upon the face
of the waters. And God said,
Let there be light: and there was light.
And God said, Let the dry land
appear: and it was so. Ahead,
not a cloud, but a mountain, foliage, sand,

and canoes putting out. Like birds
of paradise their plumes, the flash
of their wings as they crossed
the bay. Bird-men chanting the words
of Satan! Tattooed on their flesh
the mark of Cain! Are these my people? Christ

with his blood shall wash their sins away.
And what to say of that shoal
of girls, gambolling in their wake,
who climbed aboard by the bob-stay?
Such bodies, unveiled, put the soul
in peril! Dear God, see how my hands shake –

as the ship has shaken since.
Lascivious dances on the upper
deck! Foul songs to a fiddle-stick
that led our hymns! Intemperance –
and worse! Some, that last Sunday took
the sacrament, coupling in the scuppers!

The Beginning
16 April 1834

The Word was god. God: *Atua.*
Atua in my mouth. Mouth: *Fafa.*
Lord, though they mock me, yea, though they
mock Thy word; though warriors say:
How shall a man who eats his God
rebuke a man who thinks it good
to eat his enemy? they yet
shall turn from murder, take, eat
bread from a fire their idols fed.

The Contest

10 August 1834

He with his puppet, I with my *Testament*
met in the *marae*, under a breadfruit tree,
when all the chiefs and warriors were present.

He cried out: '*Te-erui* made the islands. He
made *Tahuata*.'
        I: 'Not so. There is
but one God, maker of Heaven and Earth.
He made *Tahuata* and it is His.'

He: '*Te-erui* the first man.'
                I: 'Who gave birth
to *Te-erui*?'
        He: '*O Te-tareva*.'
I: 'Whence came *Te-tareva*?'
                He: '*Avaiki*,
under all things. He climbed up and over
Tahuata.'
      I: 'Then it was here when he
climbed up?'
        He: 'Without doubt.'
                    Into my hands,
O Lord, did'st thou deliver the Priest of Baal.

I: 'How did *Te-erui* make the land
if his progenitor found hill and vale
established before his birth?'
           To this he gave
no answer. And addressing then the multitude,
I spoke of God, the Creation, Adam and Eve,
and their transgression redeemed by our Lord's blood.
Lord, let thy Sower's seed fall on good ground. Amen.

The Trials
12 March 1837

Light is come amongst them, but they
love darkness rather than light.
Five canoes I saw yesterday
put to sea southward and last night,
in a pit lined with stones, a fire
was lit, I thought, to guide them home.
Tonight, over a red sea, four
returned like moths to their tall flame
and conches bellowing round
the bay. I took my evening walk
that way, and in the firelight found
the warriors at such butcher's work
as froze my blood and now my ink.

18 March 1837

The Rodgersons will not stay:
'the island being unfit', they think,
'for civilized females'. Since they
found hideous fruit in the fork
of a tree, she has not slept. They go
next week. And I? *Yea, though I walk*
through the valley of the shadow
of death, I will fear no evil:
rather, will I rejoice
with you to guide me, Lord, and fill
my silence with an English voice.

23 August 1844

How long must these false shepherds, Lord,
seduce your flock before they feel
your rod? Another teacher lured
from school by practices most foul,
lies, popish lies! The Frenchman buys
souls with a gourd of holy water,

selling his own soul for the eyes
of Chief Totete's daughter.

18 December 1847

At Falealili. Marriage with Miss Darling

Old sobersides, is there
no more to say than that?
No praise for my bonnet,
no lament for your hat
blown overboard? Come, bless
the Lord for happiness

that your holy wooing
had not prepared me for.
Admit that your mother,
at least, would not deplore
the pleasure that we found
on her 'familiar ground'!

27 January 1855

My fever by God's grace abating, I
cut coffins until noon – the smallest one
from my own flesh for my own flesh – while my
dear partner sewed and Apu dug the grave
(breaking a mattock blade). When all was done,
we buried them in the breadfruit grove.
Eight in the earth and seven gathered round
to hear the words of comfort, which a flock
of clamorous parakeets all but drowned.
Blessed are the dead which die in the Lord.

Order from home: –

```
 1   pickaxe
 1   mattock
 1   stonecutter's chisel
 2   balls whipcord
 4   hatchets
12   yds linen
ditto lint
rose cuttings
seeds – geranium, hollyhock,
         thyme, parsley, tarragon, rosemary, mint
```

5 April 1859

He has spoken in thunder, He has stretched forth
His rod, and the wind and the waters rose
and the sun went down on His wrath.
Rain hissed along the thatch like arrows,
or what we took for rain until, at dawn,
we tasted salt and saw the sea. Our boat
it seemed must founder, or be torn
from its moorings and dashed to pieces. But
we prayed and, Faith prevailing, we forbore
to violate the Day ordained for Rest
by hauling it to safety on the shore.
All day the travail of the deep increased
as though the Last Trump should bring forth its dead.
Night fell, but not the wind and not the tide,
which roaring marched inland. The natives fled
to higher ground but nowhere could they hide
from His chastisement. As my household knelt
in prayer, the roof was blown off and we felt
beneath us three such shocks it seemed the tap-
root of the land must snap.
Out of the depths have I cried unto thee,
O Lord. Lord, hear my voice. And He gave ear,
restraining the salt wind, bidding the sea
retire. Released from the burden of fear,
my wife and children on the wet ground slept.
And I went forth to view His vengeance who
is just and merciful. The wan moon crept

from a cloud, revealing no prospect I knew
but a spectacle awful and sublime.
Taboo grove, the huts of the heathen, where
were they? All levelled: every palm tree plume
abased, every plantain root in the air,
the yam crop vanished down the ocean's throat,
our chapel and the Papist's beaten flat,
but praise God! eighty yards inland, our boat
unscarred as the Ark upon Ararat.

2 May 1859

It is God's will. Again He stretches forth
His rod, and caterpillars now complete
His punishment of a dissolute
people: *they covered the face of the whole earth,*
so that the land was darkened; and they did eat
every herb of the land, and all the fruit
of the trees which the hail had left: and there
remained not any green thing in the trees,
or in the herbs of the field, through all the land
of Egypt.
　　　　　Obscene maggot, do you dare
march even to my desk, my journal? These
have no crops for you. The pen in my hand
ploughs a poor furrow – but see – it can fill
your belly forever! God forgive me,
I have slain the agent of His will.

6 November 1859

Notes for the graveside: Sower and seed.
Our brother Apu the good ground
giving roots room, stalk strength, to bear
the swelling grain. Flour. Bread to feed
a famished people. That good ground,
harrowed, yet shall bear
His fruit an hundredfold. And I
see Apu throned in glory over us,

affirming his Master's promise
of lasting harvest. 'Let me die
the death of the righteous
and let my last end be like his.'

The Return
7 November 1859

His pen – his journal – but
the living hand that should
unite them by lamplight –
stilled under a shroud
the patchwork map of home
his mother stitched for him.

The hand that was our shield
struck down by a greater!
Husband, I cannot kneel
to praise the Creator
who with a stroke has felled
His shepherd and His fold.

The bonnet trimmed with lace
while you wrote in this book
has gone to the closet
from which, tonight, I took
the old black bonnet
with all our sorrows on it.

It and I tomorrow
and your – orphans – must they
be called – shall follow you,
but not to hear you say
'I name this child'. He cries
for me. I kiss your eyes.

16 December 1859

My dear husband, it is
finished. We are afloat
and bound for Gravesend. Once
in this cabin you wrote
your journal with the pen
I now take up again

to tell you how we left.
The brethren, visibly
affected, gave us each
a garland on the quay,
gathered in that high glade
where my two loves are laid.

You sank into the earth,
and then into the sea.
Winged spirit, protect us!
Tonight, keep watch with me
and cool the fevered limbs
of our distempered lambs.

17 December

Louisa cannot swallow.

18 December

Daybreak – Louisa gone.

20 December

At Rarotonga – laid
Sarah by William. John
gave, at the last, a cry –
'Why do you plant them?' Why!

144

NEW ZEALAND

Mother and Son
1872

Dear Johnny,
        I had such
a dream, nodding last night
over your father's charts.
We were at sea – in sight
of a mountain, foliage, sand –
you and I, hand in hand,

watching the sun come up
behind Tahuata.
To starboard, a canoe
struck sparks from the water.
In the bows – can you guess?
Arms semaphoring – yes,

your father! The canoe
came on. Paddles were shipped.
His hands reached up to me,
but in my haste I slipped
down through the green crevasse,
which closed above me as

I woke – without husband
or son, my bed as cold
as the bed of the sea.
But soon, hearing swifts scold
their young under the eaves,
I thought: they too will leave

in the wake of the sun –
my son – and with the Spring,
please God, all will return.

God in his mercy bring
my sailor – and bring them –
home to
　　　your loving M.

The Arrival
1873

My dear Mother,
　　　　　　Riding a kauri spar
I came to the New World, and ride today
kauris downriver to the hungry saw –
'What is a kauri?' I can hear you say.

　A thousand years ago it was a seed
that sprung a root the land took to its heart,
raised to a sapling slender as a reed.
Before the land existed on a chart,
its dark veins fed the dark veins of the tree
and swelled the lengthening grain, the branching crown
that lifted century by century,
as ferns and tree-ferns rose and rotted down.
In a cathedral nave not made with hands
but by the living God it took its place
and, sweetening the air with resin, stands
till the cross-cut gnaws at its base.
The pillar falls, its crown falls to the axe,
and the great trunk travels 'the rolling road'
with block and tackle and timber-jacks
to where the bullock teams take up the load
and, some miles on, the torrent that in spring
will bring it to my feet.
　　　　　　　　The creek in spate
drives the wild timber, bucking, rearing,
down to the river where we pikemen wait
to herd them into rafts. Then the slow miles –
bell-bird and mouth-organ telling the hours –

146

to Sawdust City and its howling mills.
The pistons slog. The Circular devours
the past to build a future, plank by plank.

It is a grand life, Mother. Putting half
my shilling a day in the Temperance Bank,
I shall sit by your fireside soon enough –
with a full wallet and a fob-watch on!

This piece of kauri gum brings the compressed
light of a thousand years
                              and my love
                                        John

RETURN TO SENDER. ADDRESSEE DECEASED.

A Proposal
  1874

Dear Marion,
                    I was never more
in earnest in my life
than when on the North Shore
I asked you to be my wife.
And should my prospects appear less
than your father would wish,
I have had some success
and what could not accomplish
if you would put your hand in mine –
as I have mine in His
who made the sun and moon,
the earth and all that therein is?
He will not fail me, Marion.
Say yes to Him, say yes to
                              John

A Prayer
1908

Dear God,
           Forgive me that at first,
despairing, I said 'Why
hast Thou forsaken me?' and cursed
the day that I was born. Thirty
years' labour turned to bitter smoke –
print-shop and paper store!
But later, when the morning broke
through rafters, wall, and floor,
the voice of Job at my ear said:
'The Lord gave, and the Lord
hath taken away; blessed
be the name of the Lord.'
Grant me strength and a mortgage, Lord,
and new works to proclaim
the fiery essence of Thy Word,
the glory of Thy name.

An Expostulation
1911

Father,
       Your accusations I
emphatically deny.
Was I so 'self-obsessed',
so 'blinded with self-interest': –

   When leaving school at eleven
I worked without being driven
at your machines all day?

   When at thirteen I put away
my cricket bat and football boots
and all boyish pursuits
to be your ledger clerk?

When every morning in the dark
I saddled up and rode the rounds
of Dargaville? £2
a week I saved the till
delivering *The Wairoa Bell*,
and not a thumbworn threepenny bit
did I receive for it
till I was 21.

When since, with never a 'well done'
for years of unpaid overtime,
I slaved, helping you climb
the treacherous ascent
from hustings into Parliament?

When I insured the works and drew
£600 for you
but asked not a penny
for everything the fire cost me?

Anyone reading your letter
would think me little better
than a thief. You claim
I banked your money in my name.
What are the facts? When you were called
to higher things, were all
the wages paid from Heaven?
Acting on your instructions then
I banked what came in, and paid out –
as you for years had not –
all that was due, except
to me. For 6 years I have kept
my peace, rashly believing your
best interests mine. No more.
Either you let me buy
the firm for a fair price, or I –
and half your business – leave in May.
The choice is yours.

AJ

With a Copy of Early Northern Wairoa
1916

My dear George,
           Providence has crowned
my labours in a new sphere with success.
My book is written and printed and bound.
May this first copy from the (Albion) press
divert and comfort you, calling to mind
those others far from Home who in their day
fashioned the dominion you defend.
God defend you, body and soul (they say
the French are slaves to alcohol and worse).
   We here are fighting the good fight as well.
Last month the Liquor Trade suffered a reverse,
when our petition cost the Creek hotel
its licence for disorder. This shall be
a country fit for heroes (when the Hun
is crushed) and for their children, sober, free,
serving the Lord with gladness. My dear son,
the Lord lift up the light of his countenance
upon you and give you peace now and for
evermore.
           Dad

A Couple of Field Postcards
1917

Dear Dad,
           Ta for the book.
I read it, and it came
in handy when a shell took
our Woodbines. Now your name
is on everyone's lips!
Providence, you could say
atoning for its lapse!
Don't worry. From today,

lying as low as
a tick in the wool, I'll
roll my own Wairoas
and Smile, Smile, Smile.

G.

1919

Dear Dad,

Those who subscribed
to your public fountain
may never have imbibed
a better drink than rain.
I do not mind them thinking
'Water's the best beverage',
but had I not been drinking
whisky on Vimy Ridge,
body and soul would not
today keep company.
So I'll be voting 'wet'
in the election.

G.

Congratulations
1932

Good on you, Doctor John!
To think I'd live to see
the nephew that rode on
my shoulders an M.D.
I hear you want to go
to London and folk say
'What for?' I know and so
would they, by God, if they

had fought through France – towards
the Conquering Heroes' quay-
side welcome, the fine words,
the stony section.

G.

The Return
1934

Rounding the Horn, such seas!
and at the edge of sight
always an iceberg crest.
Strapped in my bunk at night
feeling the ship drop
too far and fast to stop,

I waited for the blow,
the torn plates spouting, time
after time. But then
shuddering she would climb
out from under the wave
pouring into her grave.

If she was his patient,
my dear ship's doctor said,
he would a hundred times
have given her up for dead,
but still her pulses beat
strongly under our feet.

And entering the Bay
of Biscay, as the gale
blew out, we found a bird
exhausted on the rail –
like Noah's dove – swallow
or swift, I do not know.

Its tail a tattered flag
drooped at the stern, and yet
by that magnetic beak
the helmsman could have set
his course for Home – to which,
perhaps, it was as much

a stranger as were we.
The trumpet of the spring
was calling him, and when
he followed it, something
turned over in me, wild
and joyful, like a child.

ENGLAND

Home Thoughts from Abroad
3 September 1939

Dear Dad,
        The 9 o'clock news says 'War',
and whatever that means, it means that we're
not to see Christmas in NZ. Britain
will need – if her future is written
in flames over Warsaw – more doctors soon
than all her drawling Fortnum & Mason
heirs to brass plates in the shires. And how
shall our barbarian be schooled now?

Home Thoughts from Abroad
1955

              'The finest blades in Rome',
he told my father that first morning, 'come
from this forge. Give me a lump of your
Etruscan, Roman, Syracusan ore
and in ten years I'll have a sword for you
fit for the Emperor's side.' Scuffing a new
sandal in father's shadow, I worried
that riddle round my head – and have carried
it since like a burr. He said: 'I needn't tell
you, sir, there's more than good metal
to a good sword.' I was to learn how much.

The firing, first:
            'If a cohort can march
thirty miles in battle-order – full pack
and tools – you can walk to the baths and back
like men, not slaves.' 'Centurion, how many
miles did you march in Germany?'

If some doubted his rank, none could deny
his scars: the blue grave on his thigh
of splinters from a Parthian lance; his arms
notched with a tally of battles, night alarms,
ambushes – 'road, river, *our* line, *their* line'
sketched in the schoolyard sand. The Cisalpine
frontier burned at our backs, and its ash fell
on Rome that year and the next year as well;
ash freighting every wind, blighting one roof
in ten. The mothers of my friends wore grief
and Gaius, Marcus, and Marcellus missed
a week of school. Whenever the rest
played Romans and Barbarians, those three
would not draw lots for Spartacus and Pompey,
Caesar and Vercingetorix.
                              The years
brought back from their resonant frontiers
proconsular heroes, whose names were cut
across the blackened benches where we sat
to hear them speak of Rome . . . of her galleys
and viaducts as the earth's arteries
flowing with grain and metal . . . and of work
to be done in the eagles' endless wake.

From fire to anvil:
                     over an iron knee
we learnt the rule of law. Justice decreed
three hammer blows for bad hexameters,
four for disrespect to gods or ancestors,
five for disloyalty, six for deceit,
and one for flinching when the hammer beat.

From fire to anvil, anvil to water –
breaking its skin each morning in winter
to steel our own against the furious
skies of the frontiers awaiting us.

The frontiers of the body we pushed back,
wrestling, mapped them on the running track,
until we ruled ourselves; until, after

ten years, we were the men our fathers were.
But fired, forged, tempered, and tested, when we looked
for eagles to follow, all were plucked
naked by northern winds.
                              Today my state,
though not proconsular, is fortunate
enough. For National Servicemen with time
to kill, better the White Man's Grave than tame
parades beside the Rhine or 'bull' at home.
We do no good here and we do no harm,
as they did both, whose colours still at dawn
we hoist above the palms, at dusk haul down.
Come 'Independence', those will be laid up,
and the last legionaries played to their ship
by Hausa bugles, Ibo fifes. When quit
of us, they'll come to blows, but now all's quiet
on the Western Frontier.
                              Tomorrow,
I'm Duty Officer; tonight, must borrow
some Regular's sword for my Sam Browne.
You wonder what the sword's for? Pulling down
thunderbox lids that nobody cleans
in the Royal West African Frontier Force latrines.

Identity Parade
before the shaving mirror
1959

So, you have noticed: I am not
the man he was – the big-shot

captain of the First XV.
His jersey, cramped in polythene,

glows in my cupboard but is half
my size. Your photograph

156

shows someone else of the same name
confident before the big game.

He knows who he is and where he
is heading, but wouldn't know me

from 22925028,
the subaltern in a slouch hat.

His company in single file
threaded on a compass needle

stitch the map. He leads. He knows
at each river-bank the shallows

from the stream. If, as you tell
me, once I knew him well

we grew apart many years back.
These mornings at the eight o'clock

identity parade I am
a stranger to myself; the sum

of many strangers, who today –
since I have lost their way –

reproach me to my face. You should
get up and go shouts the blood

in my wrist – is it theirs or mine?
Without touchline or gridline

where should I go? Towards that still
mythical stranger whose stare will

appraise – commend or deride –
my choice. I can decide. Decide.

The Almond Tree
Jonathan: 1965

I

All the way to the hospital
the lights were green as peppermints.
Trees of black iron broke into leaf
ahead of me, as if
I were the lucky prince
in an enchanted wood
summoning summer with my whistle,
banishing winter with a nod.

Swung by the road from bend to bend,
I was aware that blood was running
down through the delta of my wrist
and under arches
of bright bone. Centuries,
continents it had crossed;
from an undisclosed beginning
spiralling to an unmapped end.

II

Crossing (at sixty) Magdalen Bridge
Let it be a son, a son, said
the man in the driving mirror,
Let it be a son. The tower
held up its hand: the college
bells shook their blessing on his head.

III

I parked in an almond's
shadow blossom, for the tree
was waving, waving me
upstairs with a child's hands.

IV

Up
the spinal stair
and at the top
along
a bone-white corridor
the blood tide swung
me swung me to a room
whose walls shuddered
with the shuddering womb.
Under the sheet
wave after wave, wave
after wave beat
on the bone coast, bringing
ashore – whom?
           New-
minted, my bright farthing!
Coined by our love, stamped with
our images, how you
enrich us! Both
you make one. Welcome
to your white sheet,
my best poem!

V

At seven-thirty
the visitors' bell
scissored the calm
of the corridors.
The doctor walked with me
to the slicing doors.
His hand upon my arm,
his voice – *I have to tell*
you – set another bell
beating in my head:
your son is a mongol
the doctor said.

159

VI

How easily the word went in –
clean as a bullet
leaving no mark on the skin,
stopping the heart within it.

This was my first death.
The 'I' ascending on a slow
last thermal breath
studied the man below

as a pilot treading air might
the buckled shell of his plane –
boot, glove, and helmet
feeling no pain

from the snapped wires' radiant ends.
Looking down from a thousand feet
I held four walls in the lens
of an eye; wall, window, the street

a torrent of windscreens, my own
car under its almond tree,
and the almond waving me down.
I wrestled against gravity,

but light was melting and the gulf
cracked open. Unfamiliar
the body of my late self
I carried to the car.

VII

The hospital – its heavy freight
lashed down ship-shape ward over ward –
steamed into night with some on board
soon to be lost if the desperate

charts were known. Others would come
altered to land or find the land
altered. At their voyage's end
some would be added to, some

diminished. In a numbered cot
my son sailed from me; never to come
ashore into my kingdom
speaking my language. Better not

look that way. The almond tree
was beautiful in labour. Blood-
dark, quickening, bud after bud
split, flower after flower shook free.

On the darkening wind a pale
face floated. Out of reach. Only when
the buds, all the buds, were broken
would the tree be in full sail.

In labour the tree was becoming
itself. I, too, rooted in earth
and ringed by darkness, from the death
of myself saw myself blossoming,

wrenched from the caul of my thirty
years' growing, fathered by my son,
unkindly in a kind season
by love shattered and set free.

One for the Road
May 1974

Dear Nick,
            I write this letter now
because by the time you can read
you will have forgotten how
with a new map, an old book,
and a following wind we took
the Tingewick-Preston Bissett road.
The wind had dismasted an oak – its bough

breaching the hedge its saplings thickened –
and the swifts were skiing for joy
over clouds at their journey's end:
the village to whose bright square
we returned, who had last been there
in the lurching veins of a boy
bound for the *Tuscan* lying at Gravesend.

No trace in the house of the saint
of George, his servant. But I found
in God's Acre my Red Devilment
free-falling from *James Stallworthy*
Died . . . 1773
aged 3 years. You were 3.
                        The ground
split, showing the vertiginous descent.

Envoi

June 1977

Prince of my blood, the swifts have flown
three times to Africa since then
and for your birthday now return
again. Over the churchyard, they
have been practising all day –
climb and dive, swerve and climb again –
tomorrow's festival flight-pattern.

You murmur in your sleep, as they
in theirs, while I sit polishing
my 'Mirror for a Prince', and say:
This I made for you. Find a space
among the toys in your suitcase
where it can lie, when we take wing
over the ocean to the U.S.A.

See in its warped and spotted glass
one face become another: each,
whatever its profit and loss,
eroded to familiar bone,
my father's, your father's, your own.
Lip-reading here their broken speech,
learn where you stand. Let this be your compass

and talisman. Carry it round
the world, taking your bearings from
its lines. When I was lost, I found
my way by that flickering
dark needle. So may the swift bring
you and your children's children home
to this familiar, well-planted ground.

THE ANZAC SONATA
(1986)

Counter-Attack

Returning to the biscuit tin
we could find in the dark – and often did,
hugging it in the crook of an arm,
four fingers tugging at the lid –

'It's crawling – look at it! How on earth – ?'
They crowded round, and knew, and could not say,
but it was out and crawling through the house
came where the patient lay.

'In my kitchen? Fetch me my sticks.'
As the general called for his horse,
and buttoning his tunic over his wound
rallied his levies, so she, hers.

The kettle sounded, shook its plume.
We scalded the bread-bin and scoured the floor,
under the general's terrible eye
winning the battle, if not the war.

One Day

The last morning as an immortal
passed into the last afternoon
and when the bedside lamp was lit
you told me: *Grandmother has died.*
Died?
      She has gone to Heaven.
                    When
will she be back?
      We don't come back.
We?
    Everyone goes to Heaven.
Will you go?
      One day.

                              Black lightning
scissored the wall, and the floor
fell away in a down-draught
of terror –
                    I had forgotten
that sheer shaft, the vertigo,
until the day your grandson fell
to your death and, standing astride
his darkness, I threw him
the line you lowered, wondering
when were you ever at my side
as now, my dear, my phantom limb?

The Rooms

The gown on the back of the door –
the dressing-table mirror –
the watch with arrested hands –
the tongue-tied shoes on the floor –

are waiting – but for whom?
Not that indifferent
likeness of my mother
in the other blinded room.

Defying Gravity

I can scarcely bid you good-bye, even in a letter.
I always made an awkward bow.

John Keats

Between the decorous lips
of *Henry James in Cambridge*
a book-mark lolls like a tongue
unstrung, still trying to say
something:
         Remember that day
when you, too, come to take leave;
remember reading aloud
to her, as she darned your sleeve;
remember the hands and how,
defying gravity, she rose –
'Let's leave Henry James for now' –
bending her head to receive
the last but one kiss on her brow;
making, lest you should grieve
at the curtains' perceptible close
an imperceptible bow.

The Blackthorn Spray

As the wheels of the hearse
unreeled the road
downhill, they slowed
to let the milkman pass.
His white van showed
in the black-framed glass
and the reel went into reverse.

Here the road rears
and father, setting spur
to twenty horse-power,
takes them up and over
thirty-five years,
off the edge of the map
crackling in mother's lap.

'Blue gates, the agent said –'
'We must have come too far.'
'No. There they are.'
And here is the house of the dead.
I want to stay in the car,
but not by myself under these
fluttering, muttering trees.

The lock unsealed, the door
gestures to the gloom
of corridor, corridor
and cavernous room.
Those terrible shapes!
Which dustsheet drapes
the horror in the tomb?

A soft crash, another,
as mother throws
those curtains right
and left. Light strikes
the wall like a gong,
filling the veins
of the house with song.

'If we lived here
on this hill, we might
have the wind's ear
and the sun's sight.'
Down there, in the valley
flooded now with night,
bubbles the sunk city,

but here – where am I? I'm
listening to the chime
of milk-bottles, a trilling
kettle, someone singing
arias that make
dustsheets dissolve. And I take
the stairs two at a time.

She opens doors and windows, lets
the world in. Plumage
and piano eat
from her hand, and when she plays,
the wind forgets
to turn her page,
the sun stretches out at her feet.

And in the evening, as the fire
is purring, Casals playing,
and coffee arcs from the spout,
she tells us; saying
'The x-rays leave no doubt,
but do not grieve.' The fire
burns lower, lower, out.

And night brought round the day
when hedges were in bloom
and we brought down a vision
fire would not consume –
the milk van making way
for her; the blackthorn, shaken,
scattering its spray.

Mother Tongue

At the end of the road, in a drab chapel
like an airport lounge, waiting for her flight
to be announced in five, four, three, a couple

of minutes (hear no – see no – tongues ignite),
I opened the little blue book and read:
'I heard a voice from heaven saying, Write'.

And so it was. I, too, heard what was said
and knew the voice: *Write a for apple, b
for ball* . . . Under my fist, the pencil-lead

retraced the shadow of a sound: *fat c
for cat* . . . mine was a starveling, but the sound
was shapely in her mouth. In mine, shapely

at night, the alphabet was rune and round,
an inexhaustible zodiac
whose incantation held the dark spell-bound.

The voice that every morning brought us back
to apples, and balls bouncing, brought
us to our senses, teaching us to track

the constellations of the alphabet.
I heard the voice retreating, like a bird
into a cave, and saw a silhouette

or shadow thrown by firelight, blown and blurred
against a rockface, where a line became
a lion; and the lion was transfigured

to a sign; the sign into a name.
Bone grated against stone. Above the light
insistent burr, above the tongues of flame,
I heard a voice from heaven saying, Write.

The Anzac Sonata
for Ramsay Howie, violinist

in memory
of Bill Howie, 1892-1915
and Peggy Howie, 1908-1980

Another time,
        another place.
Glossy as a conker
        in its cushioned case.

Lift and tighten
        the horsehair bow,
shuttle rosin
        to and fro.

Hold the note
        there, that first note
jubilant from
        the fiddle's throat.

I

She remembered the singing. No voice
that she knew and no words, but a cadence,
the speech of a heart with cause to rejoice.

But tell me, now sitting in silence,
with never more cause for grief,
never such darkness, such distance

between us, whether beyond belief
that speech is your speech and yours
that cause for rejoicing. And if,

beyond time, that cadence continues,
send me the jubilant echo
that came to you sixty-five years

ago. Your pen in my hand will know
the note. Its slender antenna inclines
and straightens, leans to the wall, the window.

Another time. I must learn the lines
of a window growing in a dark wall
and listen, as she, to the sibilant pines

and beyond, the approach, lapse, and withdrawal
of surf, off the Bluff, at the world's end.
Then nearer, clearer, the call
of a vibrant string. Turning as she listened,

       one cheek on the pillow
       brushed a cooler cheek
       of fragrant calico.
       Could no more – staring – speak
       than that dumb angel now
       descended here – but how –
       from the toyshop window.

       Hearing the string once more
       sing out, carried my – Nell –
       To Ramsay's room. The door
       was open. Dawnlight fell
       on bow, hand, and fiddle.
       Where did they come from?
                       Bill.
       Bill going to the War.

She remembered the drumming, a pulse in the ear
as of pounding blood, a fever shaking
schoolroom windows. She could not hear

the teacher, though her mouth was making
shapes. The drumming coming. The bell
breaking in, and as suddenly dumb.

Asphalt underfoot. She was holding Nell
in one hand; in the other, the cold
blade of a railing. The drumswell

174

swept past her leopardskin and gold,
pistons pumping thunder, and Bill
on his bay under a flag enscrolled

Otago Mounted Rifles. Then the bell
told the playground that the show
was over but, shoulder high, Nell
was still waving white calico.

Five railings down
    watching the bay
glossy as a conker
    saunter away,

groomed tail swaying
    to and fro.
Lift and tighten
    the horsehair bow.

Hold the note,
    the band's grand tune.
Hands must cup head
    all afternoon,

that not a dwindling
    chord be spilled
until the fiddle
    can be filled.

II

Good news from Gallipoli: *bought
my ticket home with a piece of lead
no bigger than a shilling . . . doctor thought
a bargain . . .* Put the best sheets on his bed.

Lift and tighten
    the horsehair bow,
shuttle rosin
    to and fro.

175

Hum and rehearse
        each afternoon
the band's grand
        jubilant tune.

Black news from Gibraltar: *died*
at sea, of fever . . . towards 5 o'clock,
pulse slackening, he went out with the tide . . .
We laid him to rest in the shade of the Rock.

A grave should be in the shade
of a tree. If we scissored
a plot in the orchard,
cut blossom, and made
a wreath, if you played
the march and I beat the drum,
would his spirit not come?

Another time,
        a brother's face.
Glossy as a conker
        in its cushioned case.

Light and tighten
        the horsehair bow.
Fingers begin,
        horse and hearse follow

under the bridge
        and varnished arch,
moving in time
        to the Dead March.

Never such darkness, such distance
between them: the one heart stilled
in its case, the other struggling for utterance.

Never such nights and such days filled
with absence – *his* bed, *his* chair – the ache
pervasive as water, and not to be spilled

in words. But stumbling fingers
take comfort from strings that sing
of another time, another place,

of hurts beyond healing, and bring
all into harmony. Music knows
what happens. The hand, bowing,

instructs the heart, as the fiddle grows
with the arm. Fernlike, its coils extend.
Hips widen. The varnish glows

with handling. They speak to each other; friend
confiding in friend, humouring, healing
the hurts. With a horsehair brush in his hand
he paints the air with the colours of feeling.

> Another time,
>> a sister's face,
> a candle shining
>> through Brussels lace.

> Lift and tighten
>> the horsehair bow.
> Let petals fly
>> and the bells blow

> under the bridge
>> and varnished arch,
> dancing to
>> the Wedding March.

She remembered the singing, the silence, the face
on the pillow. She heard the jubilant note
another time, another place.

But the angel opened its throat
and mewed for her breast. The sky she saw
reflected in its eyes seems less remote

but bluer, more miraculous than before.
The hands smell sweeter than calico,
and when the feet take to the floor

the first ant drags its shadow
into a garden where the first birds waken.
The beasts are named, and the trees also.

She saw the apple, in its season, taken
and knowing what would follow, drew
an arm through her daughter's when the road was shaken.

She knew the way. The darkness grew
transparent as they walked together.
And, when the dawn came up, she knew
her daughter older than her older brother.

III

'What did the doctor say?' She, on her bed,
could hear her heart drumming. 'He said,
"We've a bit of a battle ahead".'

Not the least cloud troubled the sky.
Heavily burdened, looking ahead,
they moved up the line to die.

  Another time,
    another place.
  Pack the fiddle
    in its cushioned case.

  Lock the door,
    take to the air.
  Fiddle and fiddler
    must be there –

  picking out
    the band's grand tune
  fiery night
    by fiery noon.

A cross-fire nailed them to the cliff
and each dug in, clawing a cave
shaped to the body that rose stiff

at first light, resurrected from its grave.
Trapped in their trenches, shelled and sniped,
with never more cause to grieve

and curse their luck, they grinned, and wiped
back bloody sweat. The steel bees
stung, but only their wounds wept.

Below them, oleanders bloomed in the gullies,
but all who dreamt of gardens woke
to harsher scents than these.

Between barbed wire and prickly oak
they held the line on the place of the skull.
Another morning broke.

In single file, they were moving downhill
and someone was singing. The sky lightened.
She – and an angel – were following Bill
to the beach – and the boat – at the world's end.

*

Another time,
    another place.
Incline the bow
    above the face

now putting out
    in a cushioned boat,
and paint a garland
    that will float

on the silence
    after her.
At the last stroke
    of the coda,

179

hold the note
    there, that first note,
jubilant from
    the fiddle's throat.

At Half Past Three in the Afternoon

On one side of the world
I was watching the waterfall
shake itself out, a scroll unfurled
against a grey slate wall,
when on the other side –
it would be half past nine, and you
in bed – when on the other side
the night was falling further than I knew.

And watching the water
fall from that hole in the sky
to be combed into foam, I caught
a glimpse in the pool's dark eye
of us, eating our bread
and cheese, watching the falling light
crash into darkness. 'Look,' you said,
'a rainbow like a dragonfly in flight.'

On one side of the world
at half past five in the afternoon
a telephone rang, and darkness welled
from a hole in the sky,
darkness and silence. Soon,
in search of a voice – how to recall
'a rainbow like a dragonfly
in flight' – I walked back to the waterfall.

The trees had lost their tongues –
as I did, coming face to face
with the glacial skeleton hung
beside our picnic place.
The spine was broken, cracked
the rib-cage of the waterfall.
The pond under its cataract
knew nothing of us, knew nothing at all.

And what did I know, except
that you, the better part of me,
did not exist? But I have kept
your anniversary
today – or there, tonight –
returning to the creek, and trying
to understand. I saw the light
falling, falling, and the rainbow flying.

Frozen Poem

Out of the silence
   a sound
somewhere
    between the white sky and white ground.

Wind in the telephone wires
   rising and falling?
A suffering hinge? Or truck tyres
   whinnying? Geese calling

up from the edge of the world
   dark words coming to light
but written rewritten rewritten
   revised and erased in flight.

Sound gone to ground, it takes root
    among flints, reaches out
shoot after whispering shoot
    till the frozen clod finds a tongue

and must speak of the nothing it knows
    but the compulsion to speak
in a language it learns as it grows,
    groping, towards an oblique

stroke on the snow. Unconstrained
    filaments, one by one,
discover the wind, as the wind
    discovers the sun, and the sun

on the roof begins drawing
    the gable's icicle teeth.
And a frozen poem, thawing,
    takes its time from the drumming beneath.

Winter was a white page

soon to be ripped
    from the calendar
      says the rippling script
        of Canada geese
          in a language
            their quills
              bring creaking
                from valleys
                  and bristling hills
                    where it entered
                      the redman's deep
                        ancestral sleep
                      a message
                      that stirred
                the bear in its bed
                the grasses
              under snow
          a message heard
          and read
        at an open
        window
      by one
      whose
    pen
    passes
  the
word

Windfalls

There are stars in the grass,
Orion behind
the apple tree. I'll find
a jam jar and a glass

and, kneeling in the dark
where amorous fireflies,
catching each other's eyes,
speak with a tender spark,

I'll fill an indoor sky
with fallen starlight –
enough, at least, to write
a love poem by.

Making a Bed

for Jill after twenty years

We have three sorts of bed
Plato, *The Republic*

God made the first – in a dreamwork-shop
behind the bicycle leaning on the nose
of the carpenter from Minsk. Straight from the snows
of childhood, it came to a jingling stop.

Take off the runners and there you are:
curved footboard, scalloped for reins,
curved headboard, crested and carved
with bells – a bed fit for a tsar

and tsarina. The carpenter took wood
and under his gauging thumb it grew
towards the troika-bed that you
and I tested and found good.

So why make another? A spare bed
may have its uses: as when one,
at the end of a day, having eaten and done
the dishes, remembers the other head

on the other pillow, and can resume
the broken journey, riding to sleep,
breathing in unison, breathing deep,
twin plumes braided in a single plume.

Making a Table
for Jack Rosco

The bird that dropped the cherry stone
set in slow motion on the air
ripples extending ring on ring,
ascending spring on spring to where
the bird was when it dropped the stone.

The bird was dust before the grain
reversed the rain's flow to the ground,
before the men came with the saw,
men who were dust before we found
a table shadowed in the grain.

As you for me, so I for you
measured my lengths and matched the grain,
ripple to ripple. Wordshavings fell
from the tongue's lathe and the pen's plane,
and one shape grew from many for you.

Draw up a chair as I draw the cork
of this first bottle, and drink a toast
to those converging, who will arrive
at this round table when we are dust,
will draw a chair up, draw a cork,

and debating the nature of things
will celebrate circularity,
the coming together of wood and word,
the coming together of you and me,
the eternal convergence of things.

For Zhenia Yevtushenko
who translated 'The Almond Tree' into Russian

I made my son a poem
under an almond tree
shadowing me in him,
shadowing him in me,

and we three at home
lived happily until
one day the poem
walked out as children will,

since when, sometimes, somewhere,
hearing a voice I know
and stopping then to stare,
I thought 'my son', but now,

since you have taught it Russian
under another tree,
I think of grandchildren
I shall not hear or see.

For Margaret Keynes
1890-1974

1 *With love and eighty candles, 1970*

Margaret, born to the flawless summers
And skies that only birds could climb, a low
Rustle of legends attends you now,
Going round your garden with secateurs
And trug, while astronauts walk on the moon . . . .
Remembered, many a brilliant head
Excitedly talking: your own excited
To hear new leaves dancing to an old tune.

Keeper of a wisdom ancient as the heart,
Embodied in the sure, whole-hearted way
You tend a grandson's knee or mend a shirt,
Nurture a plant or write a letter, few
Ever lit more candles for others. May
Spring light many more crocuses for you.

2 *With love and winter jasmine, 1974*

Dear Margaret,
                                Now four years later,
Because the chronicle must be kept
Complete and the chronicler overslept,
I think I should write you a letter
Telling you how it went. It was your kind
Of day: the sun up first, drying the eyes
Of puddles in the lane; the Suffolk skies
And corduroy ploughlands clean swept by the wind.

The church full, as for harvest festival
(Such corn-haired grandchildren!), heard the old words
Who would true valour see and *For all*
The saints sung (flat) by those who later, dumb
Beside a furrow crossed by singing birds,
Gave thanks for harvests gathered and to come.

187

In Memory of Geoffrey Keynes KT
late of Lammas House
1887-1982

When wing to wing, feather by feather,
the rooks were piecing night together,
I took the ring the iron-lipped
iron-lidded lion gripped
and tapped the call-sign on his hide.
He knew me, nodded, moved aside,
and as the light fell through the door
I walked into your head once more.

I could distinguish, layer by layer,
each constituent of the air:
vellum and beeswax; apple, oak,
and elm gone up in years of smoke;
tanned pastry, ghosts of roasted meat;
the breath of oxlips, wintersweet,
jasmine, and Stanley Spencer's tall
corinthian hyacinths on the wall.

The old clock in a fancy waist-
coat cleared its throat and, poker-faced,
pointed to Margaret's room. I must
have slipped in without sound or gust,
for on the mantelpiece the frieze
had thawed and bountiful Ceres
bowed from a festal chariot drawn
by cherubs shouldering sheaves of corn

for Lammas. Darwin in a chair
inhaled his beard. And through a pair
of ancient spectacles, tugged free
from a book's teeth, I could see
a knickerbockered boy advance
to greet a flock of bustled aunts.
The clock struck. They went out like flames –
leaving their shadows, shrunk, in frames.

And I went also, up the stairs
where Catharine Blake's embroidered hares
danced in the moonlight. Ran a bath
under the gaze of a lithograph,
'Sixty-four Years a Queen', to whom
I bowed: 'Allow me to presume
to higher strains if you will use
it first, ma'am.' 'We are not a muse.'

And so to such a downy bed
and downy pillow that the head
no sooner settled . . . than today
came in with teacups on a tray.

But not today, and not again
the day sketched over the counterpane,
an airy canvas, to be swept
with sunlight in a south transept,

and more than sunlight as we walk
through Danes' Blood, welling from the chalk,
or in the workshop carve those two
owl-guardians of your gateposts, who
today, frock-coated mourners, keen
for you as we process between.
Your books cry your name from the shelf,
but where's your masterpiece – Yourself?

Not in your house, or over there
in Brinkley churchyard's flinty loam.
The rooks return, return and riot,
the rooks return and you do not.
I shall know where to find you, how-
ever, for ever. Old master, now
that your fire's out, draw up a chair
to mine, and make yourself at home.

Goodbye to Wilfred Owen

killed, while helping his men
bring up duckboards, on the
bank of the Sambre Canal.

After the hot convulsion, this
cold struggle to break free – from whom?
I am not myself nor are his
hands mine, though once I was at home
with them. Pale hands his mother praised,
nimble at the keyboard, paler
now and still, waiting to be prised
from wood darker for their pallor.

Head down in a blizzard of shrapnel,
before the sun rose we had lost
more than our way. Disembodied
mist moves on the goose-fleshed canal,
dispersing slowly like the last
plumed exhalations of the dead.

Wiedersehen
for Joachim Utz

Tom – and in time! I never thought you'd come
or not in time, since that's in short supply.
They can't plug an hourglass into my arm,
but no matter now. You're here, and I
must find the words whose loss cost me your love.
What do I know of loss? Do you deny
your 'unforgiving father' knowledge of love?
Of anything but hatred? When I tried
to stop you learning German, would not have
your *Freunde* in the house, your *Fräulein*, bride –
not even her – that was no hatred, or
no hatred of Germans. Sit beside

190

the bed. I'll tell you a story.
                                    The war
had reached the Rhineland and a riverbank
where a blown bridge knelt in the water.
The first soldier to reach it knelt and drank
and was shot in the head. A second, hit
lifting him, crashed in the river, sank.
Six crowded in a ditch. One raised his helmet
on a stick and it clanged like a bell
holed by a high velocity bullet.
A sniper, and in front, among the rubble
once a village on the other shore.
The officer went left – then right – bent double
down the ditch, and gave his orders: 'Four
men, left – together at the ditch's end
dash for the farmhouse and return his fire;
two to go right – the ditch follows the bend
in the river, swim across, and ambush him.'
The Old'un led off his unblooded friend,
the Young'un, right. The bren snarled after them
and the sniper replied. Rounding his flank,
they came to the river. Rifles can't swim
so they strapped them each to a driftwood plank
and ferried them over. It was so cold,
the water and the wind on that scoured bank,
their fingers bled before they unbuckled
their guns and could move on – each covering
the other – to the kill, or to be killed.
Only a bird stirred in the lane, shivering
as they, sidling from tree to tree, shivered,
and then from doorway to doorway. Turning
into the square, the Old 'un never heard
the shot that starred his face. The Young'un backed
against a door. It opened, and he entered
retching; from a reflex of a cracked
shop window, saw the church across the square,
its chancel smouldering, its belfry hacked
away, a tower beheaded, but there
above the parapet a moving head.
Hatred raised the rifle to the shoulder,

aligned the sights and braced the arm. Hatred,
hardly breathing, beckoned. As the muzzle leaped
the man stood up, and with his arms outspread
could have been crucified – until he stepped
into thin air.
                    He wore no uniform,
no bandolier. You would have thought he slept
but for his eyes, and his black coat was warm
to the touch of hands in search of papers. None,
except the photograph: he had his arm
around the waist of a woman,
who held a boy's hand and the flaxen plait
of a girl.
                    Why do you look at me like that?
In God's name, what are you staring at?

At St Gennys

In their grandmothers' footsteps, the girls
of St Gennys played Grandmother's Footsteps
and skipped, skipped, in a blossom of curls
and pinafores, while the boys snatched caps
and shied them over the churchyard gate,
till Miss shook her bell to quell the noise
and call them in to chalk-stub and slate
through the door marked GIRLS and the door marked BOYS.

With a key from the cottage we let ourselves in
(through the door marked GIRLS) to the long room
empty since . . . Empty? Cupboard doors open
on a coiled adder, guardian of the tomb.
A gasp laughed off, seeing the eye unlit,
my sons drift out to swing on the farm gates.
And warily I lift the corselet
from the hoard, a stack of children's slates.

I cannot read the Book of the Dead,
but hear scribes breathing, a chalk edge
etching the darkness from which, now, a head
lifts, looking beyond the window-ledge,
the ivy tendril, and the churchyard wall –
to what enlightenment? How time translates
chalk-written names and tots up all
our stumbling numbers into frozen dates?

Not many, I think, learnt translation here.
But was there a sprouting boy who did not
look to that window, colouring its clear
glass with his dreams? What fish? What fairgrounds? What
sealed orders from the girls' sealed lips
sailed past the church tower, and what cargo
was there for them when their ships
came home? Their grandchildren would know.

Or would have known, had not three bachelors
of this parish dunged a field in France;
three more gone, weighted, to the fishes' jaws;
one fallen like a star. Five spinster aunts,
sometimes when tossing the sheaves from stook
to cart, would break off, brushing a strand
of hair back from their eyes, and look
out to cloud convoys making for the land.

Great Britain

Out of what depths the dream?
Compounded of what elements? How long
that slow growth, swelling a seam
to ripeness, reconciling
fire and water, earth and air? Under
its own power, now it strikes up, a song
in search of words, a theme for thunder,
overture to a new age, the rising dream of STEAM!

Isambard Kingdom Brunel
heard it above the sounding brass
pounded round a table in Radley's Hotel.
Motions proposed, pass
and fail. Air thickens with the word 'Expand'
scrolled in calculations scrawled by cigars.
'Why should the line end with the land?
Extend it to New York with a steamboat out of Bristol.'

Shipwrights take up the theme,
orchestrating the *Great Western*
till paddle-wheels churn at her beam,
black and white at the stern
shrink to a smudge. Oscillating pistons pound
the sun's track outward, turn and return.
Trumpets sound as a queen is crowned.
Brunel's divining pencil hovers above the dream:

a bridge between old and new,
two piers and a single span
sustaining the traffic of nations. He drew
a line. A second ran
to meet it. Contours of bow, counter and beam
came clear in a flurry of notes. African
oaks crashed to the axe, but the voice of the dream
demanded not timber but iron, not paddles but a screw.

With spirit-level and line,
hod and trowel, back and forth,
bricklayers build to Brunel's design
a mammoth womb for a mammoth.
Naysmith works on his steam-hammer, the plate-maker's forge
lights up. Iron seeds jerked from Shropshire earth
enter the crucible, merge, emerge
in a dry dock, marrow cells of a mammoth spine.

Rib after rib now
rises to be sheathed in an iron skin
by riveters swarming from sternpost to prow,
     whose fusillade brings in
the Royal Salute, trumpet and fife and drum.
Ten thousand top hats go off in every direction
     at a word from the Prince, who swings a magnum
against the shifting cliff. Lion and Unicorn bow

     and lead out, inscrolled
on a trailboard, dove, caduceus, trumpet
and lyre, wheatsheaf and gearwheels of gold.
     Roll out the red carpet!
Flags, speak with tongues! Bandmaster, play
Rule Britannia! Fireman, shake sweat
     from your eyes and believe them. Say
to your children: 'As God is my witness, the Queen in my stokehold!'

     The heart quickens its beat
and six masts sing as one
as Lion and Unicorn rise to meet
     the concerted assault of the ocean;
     as the immigrant stands at the stern, tight-lipped;
     as the chef in the galley cuts cucumber scales for a salmon;
     as the captain writes in a copperplate script
'eleven knots'; and the world turns under their feet.

     Eighteen forty-six.
Off-guard, the ship, ripped by the claws
of Dundrum Bay, jarred by its jaws,
     breaks the teeth that transfix
her, throws coal to the sea and scrawls *Help*
on the sky – until dawn calls the tide off. Passengers,
     praising God, flounder through kelp
and bog with their lives in their hands. But the *Great Britain* sticks

all winter in the Irish gizzard.
Come summer, come levers, come pulleys and weights,
wedges and screw-jacks. A hammer-struck chord
on $\frac{3}{4}$ inch plates
leads back the music of the dream. She rises to the tide.
The capstan breaks into song. The cable grates
as she warps herself off. From Merseyside,
a gun-salute greets the lamed Unicorn's call; and, at Liverpool, word

from Australia: the word was *gold*.
Refitted, rerigged, she takes aboard
the younger son, the crofter, the farmer who sold
his farm, and plunging southward
holds a long mirror to their dream, that sudden gleam
threading the broken wave. A few of them roared
with the Forties home, voices of steam
and cigar smoke boasting of bullion in the safe and cotton in the hold.

Iron voices now
break in, trumpet snarling at trumpet,
the battle-cry of the Lion at the bow,
as jingling files of scarlet
stamp aboard at Liverpool, ashore at Scutari.
Winds threaten. Another course set
for the Cape and Bombay, she carries a battery
of guns, a squadron of lancers, for Cawnpore and Lucknow.

The world turns under her keel
though the screw turns no longer under the wave.
A windjammer with her holds full of coal,
she runs for the Horn and the grave
gapes as a hurricane hammers her. Topgallants crack,
decks leak, and she lists, till her shifting coal
shovelled uphill, she limps back
To Port Stanley, a listless hulk in her last haven

but one. *Nineteen-fourteen.*
Sturdee's ships, loading coal
from her, stop, as *Scharnhorst* and *Gneisenau* are seen.
Gruff echoes roll
round the bay, startling the seals, but the Lion never blinks.
The Unicorn utters no cry, as the scuttling hole
is struck and the *Great Britain* sinks
in her own reflection. Now circling seabirds keen

no longer, for she
has risen, come clear
of her winding sheet, with all her gear
shining, as at first he
divined her, Isambard Kingdom Brunel.
A lesser bard takes up his tune. See here,
a ship in a bottle, a translucent shell,
that held to the ear inland, remembers the pulse of the sea.

THE GUEST FROM THE FUTURE
(1995)

The Nutcracker
For Isaiah Berlin

My story? Yes, I got my story
though not the one I was assigned.
It was a Voyage of Discovery
all right, but of another kind.
The latest Russian Revolution
was no sooner known than it – *woosh* – un-
corked Moscow like shaken champagne,
filled Red Square to the brim again
with chanting thousands. When Apollo
appeared on the balcony, they
let out a shout heard miles away.
He made a speech I couldn't follow
but knew would be a press release
before I had to write my piece.

A theme for Shostakovich: Russia's
Columbus, orbiting the earth
alone for 90 minutes, ushers
the space-age in. At such a birth
Siberian stars should sing hosannas,
not children with *Gagarin* banners.
Flags licked his face all afternoon.
Later, beneath a carnival moon,
I went to someone's celebration
and there, at the turn of a head,
a whisper, I was rocketed
beyond hope – dread – imagination –
I'm telling this the wrong way. I'm
afraid I must go back in time

before the war, to days we've chosen
not to discuss. Imagine me
emerging – into air like frozen
vodka – from the *wagon-lit*
at Moscow station. January
of 1938. A very
far cry from the *Champs Elysées,*

les croissants dans le petit café,
a pipe and *Le Temps*, a part in a
continuous historical play
I was helping to write all day,
white-tie reception, black-tie dinner,
five-star brandy and five-star dreams:
a canter in the *Bois* . . . *Maxims* . . .

So there I was in a dim Chancery,
all day the very model of
a modern Second Secretary,
reviewing files on Molotov
or drafting, when the show-trial circus
began, reports on how the workers
of Krasnoyarsk had been betrayed.
Eyes in the courtroom were afraid
and not in the courtroom only,
but in the streets, the trams that hurled
them home at dusk and left the world
to darkness and the N.K.V.D.
I turned in early, took to bed
Memoirs from the House of the Dead.

A thunderous summer, a long winter,
though there'd be longer. Spain ablaze
and Britain refusing to inter-
vene. Now, it's not the last red days
of Barcelona I remember
so much as finding, in December,
a glint of green. Not in the park,
but in a studio after dark
where champagne bottles fountained freely,
toast after toast. Somebody said
'Tatyana'. Laughter, and a head
was turned. 'Tatyana Taraschvili.'
Her eyes were champagne-bottle green,
the greenest eyes I'd ever seen.

And her voice had a champagne sparkle
in it: 'You are a diplomat
of course.' My diplo-patriarchal
amour propre was piqued by that.
'And you?' I said. 'A fortune-teller?'
'No.' 'Actress?' 'No.' 'A teacher?' 'No.' 'Well, a
translator?' 'No.' The man beside
her smiled at her as she replied,
and picked up an accordion. Swaying
a little and tapping one toe,
he started playing – a low
slow pulse – advancing and delaying.
Tatyana said, 'Will you excuse
me please?' and stepped out of her shoes.

The drinkers and the talkers, hearing
the music, fell back to the wall
and she stepped forward into the clearing
and stopped, making no move at all.
What started as the first faint stirring
of summer wind, the murmuring
of birches, rocked the orchards, made
the barley sway. And she soon swayed.
Then glided off with small steps stitching
the edge of the clearing, white feet
obedient to the steady beat.
She was Daphne. She was bewitching!
The accordion caught its breath, changed key.
Apollo was bewitched – like me.

She danced a *pas de deux* with her shadow,
embroidering the smokey air
as if the law of gravity had no
imperial jurisdiction there,
but other winged heels crossed the meadow.
The music quickened. A tornado
all but plucked her off the ground,
spinning round and faster round
and faster round, with arms extended,
and every time I crossed her line

of vision, green eyes engaged mine.
When, with a chord, the whirlwind ended,
a storm of clapping shook the eaves
but not the laurel with two green leaves.

I had my answer. She was toasted
again, again, again. More chords,
and everybody danced, or most did.
A lamp was swaying and floor-boards
shuddered at Cossack leaps. My *Dashing
White Sergeant* sent their glasses smashing
against the wall, but there were more.
We gravitated to the floor
as the liquor found its level
and launched a song with a song in tow
like Volga barges deep and slow.
Tomorrow could go to the devil!
Meanwhile, champagne, accordion –
On with the dance! Tatyana? Gone.

Prince Charming had a hangover
the size of an onion dome
and no tall footman to discover
the barefoot Cinderella's home.
But *was* she – champagne's a deceiver –
Natasha Rostov *rediviva*?
I had to find her to know that.
Some mornings after, as I sat
considering coffee and a stiff tot
of whisky, came a letter: *Dear
dashing white British Grenadier,
have you outgrown toy soldiers? If not,
come with this ticket and enjoy
the Nutcracker at the Bolshoi.*

I went of course, and when the curtain
swept back a century to show
the candled Christmas tree, I'm certain
no child at the darkened window
so caught its breath. 'Is it her? Is it her?'

I asked of each elegant visitor
in velvet and long white gloves.
The children eddied round like doves
with Masha in the lead. And Masha –
for all the turbulent cascade
of hair remembered in a braid –
was unmistakably Natasha.
Watching the wave of her hair,
I knew she knew that I was there.

At midnight in her dream – or was it
my dream? – when all the guests had gone,
the Mouse King marched from the closet
and with his brigand battalion
attacked the grenadiers. Surrounded,
outnumbered, the toy soldiers sounded
their trumpets, fought and fell, until
all but the Nutcracker lay still.
They cut him down, had stabbed and kicked him,
when Masha flashed across the room
and with a well-aimed slipper boom-
eranged the King. Raising his victim,
her kisses and her tears transformed
the wooden limbs her body warmed.

Her prince I didn't warm to greatly –
the rippled hair, insistent smile.
He handled her too intimately
for someone known such a short while,
but he danced well – she danced superbly –
and their *rapport* did not disturb me
for, as she danced with him, I thought
she danced for me. Then as he brought
her, gliding in his magic troika
through waltzing snowflakes, waltzing flowers,
I thought 'the Last Waltz could be ours'.
Naive! But after the Bolshoi cur-
tain closed, Tchaikovsky in my head
sent me waltzing home to bed.

Next day – one of those Saturdays a
man feels the world and the flesh in tune –
my face met a waltzing razor,
my coffee a waltzing spoon.
I reined my pen in as it wrote her
a note that showed not one iota
of what I wanted it to say,
but *Thank you . . . magical . . . and may
I have the pleasure, etc.,
on New Year's Eve?* She came, her bloom
irradiating my grey room.
The bortsch was good, the wine was better,
a candle flame danced in the draught,
pirouetting when we laughed.

How far that little candle . . . laughter . . .
Tatyana's exuberant mime!
We talked the Old Year out, and after
our glasses had sounded their chime,
we talked the New Year in. I drove her
home when the night was almost over;
or almost home, lest we should meet
the N.K.V.D. in her street.
'Next time,' she said, 'I'll do the cooking.'
Leant over, kissed me. The car door
slammed in the wind. She turned the cor-
ner, collar up, without looking
back, and before I could move on,
her footprints, filled with snow, had gone.

Another wait, another letter.
Five days, four evenings – three, two, one –
returning to Tchaikovsky's meta-
morphosis, a transformation
no more miraculous, no greater
than mine, to other music, later.
After my Bollinger's salute
to her triumphant *boeuf en croûte,*
when first the electricity
and then the candle failed, what could

we do? At least the stove had wood
enough. When snow had put the city
to bed, what could we do, discov-
ering (what else?) we were in love?

With that, our music changed key, quickened.
We danced through January, danced
through February. Birch buds thickened –
and headlines, as Hitler advanced
on Prague. We danced, one night in March, a
snowflake waltz to a borrowed *dacha* –
my Humber waltzing down the road
to Peredelkino. It snowed
all that weekend. We didn't bother,
but stayed luxuriously in bed.
Ourselves an open book, we read
Eugene Onegin to each other
and thanked our stars that they were not
Eugene and his Tatyana's lot.

How could we doubt, ecstatic lovers,
that ours were dancing night and day
in some Chagall-like zone above us
as April melted into May,
snow into blossom? Every Sunday
we woke in a world of Sugar Candy
at Peredelkino, and there
forgot that other stars elsewhere
were goose-stepping to music harsher
than ours. In the world we left behind,
Hitler and Mussolini signed
a treaty, Germany and Russia
announced a non-aggression pact,
and then the fear became the fact.

But still we danced – despite the writing
emerging on the Chancery wall
where moving fingers flagged the fighting –
until, in '41, the wal-
tzing stopped. In the blink of an eyelid,

a telegram, two worlds collided.
I was recalled. What could I do?
I could resign, and did. I knew
a London newspaper that wanted
a Man in Moscow, and applied.
I had (I said) sources inside
the Kremlin. So I was appointed,
bar the formalities, and flew
to England for an interview.

There was no interview. I landed
as Russia caught fire from the Black
Sea to the Baltic. I was stranded –
no job, no visa, no way back –
conscripted, between ice and fire.
My letters to Tatyana (via
the diplomatic bag) brought no
reply. Her footprints filled with snow,
snow burying a U-boat chaser
off Archangel, the snows of four
pitiless winters. When the war
was over, I went back to trace her.
Found nothing but a bombed-out flat.
Came home. Found you. And that was that –

until this week, that celebration.
The turn of a head. Those eyes.
My name with an intonation
not heard for 20 years. Replies
to 20 years' interrogation:
'Leningrad . . . through the siege . . . starvation . . .
the survivors had someone for whom
to survive.' She looked across the room
and smiled – at *him*. Daybreak and tidal
wave! Drowning, I saw us again –
dancing, cooking, drinking champagne,
reading, waking – and then as I'd al-
ways dreamt we'd be: husband and wife,
father and mother. Child. A life

usurped. I saw him, the usurper,
their *pas de deux* a shuffle ov-
er snow, their scavenging for supper,
resuscitating a cold stove.
I saw them in the white nights, under
one blanket, hearing the guns thunder
and plaster trickle down the wall.
Untrue. I saw nothing at all,
heard nothing, would not taste those kisses
and tears. I was lost in the wake
of their lives. Then felt Tatyana take
my hand and heard her saying: 'This is
your son.' So there it is, my story.
And I'm so happy. I'm so sorry.

The Girl from Zlot
For Jade Drysz

> *Four gray walls, and four gray towers*
> *Overlook a space of flowers,*
> *And the silent isle embowers*
> > *The Lady of Shalott.*
> > > Alfred, Lord Tennyson

1

Mile after dark Silesian mile
the river wears the forest's frown,
only venturing a smile
to greet a village or a town:
   one on an island, where
four grey walls and four grey towers
see the patients come and go,
and sufferers in the small hours,
hearing a voice beside them, know
   the girl from Zlot is there.

Midnight: an emergency:
at the operating table,
opposite the surgeon
she draws as deft a needle,
   ties as neat a knot.
When screens are drawn about a bed,
voices lowered and feet swift,
a sick child or a wounded
miner on his final shift
   asks for the girl from Zlot.

Off duty, climbing a grey tower
and in her attic opening
a window on the lights below her,
she stands a moment listening –
   listening for what?
Water talking to the wharves,
wind to rushes; rowlocks – a late
fisherman – where the river curves

carrying its nightly freight
of longing down to Zlot.

She strikes a match. The lamp
ripens and irradiates
folds of linen in her lap,
a border she illuminates
   with a needle dipped
in silk. She has a mind to make
a bedspread Book of Hours, and here
in her dipping hand's slow wake
pictures of the world appear:
   her world, her manuscript.

First, a workshop: workbench, wall,
and a carpenter who stands
catching a window's waterfall
in a box between his hands.
   He made it, matched the grain
of oak or elm (as she, its shade
of brown, the window's blue and green).
He dovetailed the four sides, inlaid
the lid. And in her second scene
   he holds his box again.

A gipsy fiddler and a lad
hugging an accordion
must be playing fast and loud
to keep these couples dancing. One,
   only one is not.
It is a guardsman and his girl.
The present he is giving her,
his broad clear brow and coal-black curls,
show him to be the carpenter,
   and she? The girl from Zlot.

Third, an attic: table, chair,
orange moon and lemon lamp
shining on a woman's hair.
She has something in her lap.

Her right hand reaches out
for something on the table –
a box her hand will enter
in search of thread or thimble
given by the carpenter
    to the girl from Zlot.

2

There by night her needle flickers
in the margin of her days
till summer-lightning swastikas
scissor the August haze.
    One morning she comes down
in a headscarf and a frock,
wheels her cycle out and shakes
across the cobbles, past the dock,
over the owl-eyed bridge, and takes
    the Zlot road out of town.

The river keeps her company.
Low and slow it holds its peace.
Riding high and rapidly
along the bank beneath the trees,
    she sings to feel the earth
freewheeling, the wind flattering;
to discover in the shade
of the vaulted colonnade
a remote sun scattering
    its petals in her path.

The river keeps her company
with its barges and the men
shouting 'Tow us home, honey',
lifting briar funnels when
    she waves and answers 'Not
today.' The miles unwind. She leaves
forest and towpath. Fields away,
weary reapers, piling sheaves,

hear her singing, stop, and say:
    'There goes the girl from Zlot.'

Two closer voices clutch her heart:
an old man talking to a horse
and the grumble of a cart
lurching from rut to rut. They pause.
    Cashtanka at the trot,
mane shaking, brings the last
of the harvest and with it,
as so often in the past,
her master and her favourite
    jingling home to Zlot.

Of the young men who last year
helped them shift the load and stack it,
only one today is here
(with a leave-pass in his jacket).
    At tables set with flowers
they eat their harvest supper, sing
the old songs under the old moon
until sleep enters harvesting
the harvesters – for two, too soon
    to share their Book of Hours.

Up at dawn and arm in arm
strolling to the river-bank
they hear the rumble of a storm,
feel the earth shake, see a tank
    break cover, growling. Squat,
reptilian, a second, third,
fourth, fifth, sixth, seventh snouting head
sniffs the wind, and then a herd
of lorries. 'Those are Germans,' said
    the carpenter from Zlot.

Instead of petals, bloodstains starred
her path, and more than stubble burned
next day. A pulse was thudding, scarred
sky shrieking. And as she returned

across the bridge, she thought:
*If I come through today, tonight
I have my Book of Hours, our bed-
spread.* Then, *But how can I delight
in pictures when he may be dead?*
    wondered the girl from Zlot.

3

Four grey walls and four grey towers
saw the stretchers come and go
and walking wounded at all hours
file across the blackened snow.
    She saw them also, not
with her eyes only, but renewed
through a third, unblinking eye.
These by lamplight had reviewed
linen snow and linen sky
    the night she heard the shot.

She left her needle, left her room.
She saw the swastikas, she saw
the helmets' and the jackboots' bloom,
the Lüger in the leather claw,
    the doctor sprawling, dead.
'Are you in charge?' The girl from Zlot
nodded, mirroring the man's
blue stare. 'Civilians? I think not.
Which of these are partisans?'
    the *Oberleutnant* said.

'None of them,' she answered. 'Then
lead us to the morgue,' he said,
turned, and beckoning his men,
followed the Polish nurses, led
    by the girl from Zlot.
Ten coffins on a flagstone floor.
In front of each a woman stands.
'Listen. I will ask once more:

Which of those are partisans?
    Remember or be shot.'

'There is nothing to remember,'
said the girl from Zlot. 'Turn round,'
the *Oberleutnant* ordered them.
'Lay your coffin-lids on the ground
    and then get into bed.'
But when they raised the lids they saw
a Polish or a German head.
The baffled Lüger looked at the floor
and the living looked at the dead.
    'Get back upstairs,' he said.

Four grey walls and four grey towers
saw Russians come and Germans go
and visitors with food or flowers,
epiphanies that she would sew.
    And sights the sick forgot
in sleep, or struggled to forget,
she remembered and set down
by candlelight until the night
she had visitors of her own,
    two visitors from Zlot.

The years since they had gathered flax,
cooked harvest suppers and made lace
together, had left panzer-tracks
on the older woman's face,
    but in their caves of bone
her eyes were smiling. 'He has sent
two hundred Deutschmarks for a guide
to bring you to his regiment,
if you want to be his bride,
    inside the Allied Zone.'

'Your embroidery is nice,
very nice,' the peddler said.
'In winter my cross-country price
is not two but three hundred,

215

but GIs pay a lot
for nice embroidery.
Remember that I risk my life.
You have no money, and would he
prefer a present or a wife?'
  he asked the girl from Zlot.

4

All that day it had been snowing,
and at twilight in the woods
shifting drifts made heavy going
for the three in sheepskin hoods
  ghosting towards – what –
freedom or a foot-patrol?
The peddler led and at the back,
shouldering a bedding-roll
as the man in front a pack,
  stumbled the girl from Zlot.

'They watch the river. Last week, twice,
men were machine-gunned as they crossed
silhouetted on the ice,
but the tall pine on that crest
  overlooks a spot
of open water.' There she found
a floating branch, to which she roped
her bedding-roll, and looking round
kissed the flinty wind she hoped
  was blowing towards Zlot.

Drifts were smoking – the wind, white –
water, black. As she slid in,
slant snow hid the men from sight.
She heard nothing but the wind
  until she heard the shot,
the shout, more shooting, shouting, then
nothing but the wind. A torch-
beam trawled the river, trawled again

across and back, but failed to catch
    the swimming girl from Zlot.

Death was reaching out his hand
underwater when she thought,
'I would rather die on land'
and, reaching our her own hand, caught
    a root and crawled ashore.
Nothing but the wind was there
offering an eiderdown,
which she shook off, and woodsmoke – where?
Following its scent, at dawn
    she knuckled a farmer's door.

Faces came and went above her
in a feverish parade:
the *Oberleutnant* and her lover,
moving lips that made
    no sound. Though she could not
move hand or foot, forest and field
came and went before her eyes.
Then she knew that she was sealed
in a coffin carved from ice
    and floating down to Zlot.

Resurrected, in a bed
draped with her embroidery,
'How long have I been here?' she said.
'A week? That leaves me less than three
    to get where I have got
to be.' When she could lift her load,
they let her go – into the wind
and snowdrifts of the longest road
ever travelled or imagined
    by the girl from Zlot.

On the last night of the year
in a lighted station, packed
with refugees, he stooped to peer
at huddled bundles with a cracked

suitcase and cooking pot.
Her life was an open book
when he found her curled asleep,
and kneeling, reading, weeping, took
her in his arms and to his jeep
  carried the girl from Zlot.

The Guest from the Future
a triptych
1940-1988
Leningrad-Tashkent-Moscow-Oxford

FOREWORD

In November 1945, Isaiah Berlin, then First Secretary at the British Embassy in Moscow, was visiting Leningrad and learnt from a conversation in a bookshop that Anna Akhmatova was living nearby. Telephoned, she invited him to call at her flat in the old Fontanny Palace on the Fontanka. Their meeting that afternoon was interrupted, as he describes in his *Personal Impressions*: 'Suddenly I heard what sounded like my first name being shouted somewhere outside. I ignored this for a while – it was plainly an illusion – but the shouting became louder and the word "Isaiah" could be clearly heard. I went to the window and looked out, and saw a man whom I recognized as Randolph Churchill. He was standing in the middle of the great court, looking like a tipsy undergraduate, and screaming my name.' Berlin hurriedly led him away, but himself returned that evening to continue his conversation with the poet. They talked all night of their respective Russian childhoods, of such of her early friends as Modigliani and Salomé Andronikova, of the war, of Tolstoy, of what she had written – and read him – of 'Poem without a Hero'. In the small hours of the morning they were joined by her son, Lev Gumilev, bringing the only food they had in the flat. This meeting, because of Churchill's interruption, came to Stalin's attention ('So our nun is receiving visits from foreign spies'), altering the course of Akhmatova's life and, she believed, the course of history. She became convinced that, fuelling Stalin's paranoia, they had caused the first move in the Cold War.

Berlin came to say goodbye to her, before leaving the Soviet Union, on 5 January 1946. The next day, uniformed men screwed a microphone into her ceiling. That summer she was denounced by the Central Committee of the Communist Party and expelled from the Writers' Union. On 6 November 1949, her son Lev was arrested for the third time and the following day Akhmatova committed her poems finally to memory before burning their manuscripts; among them, the completed 'Poem without a Hero' in which Berlin appears as 'The Guest from the Future'.

219

1

The doorbell   a tocsin   tolling
as if the Huns were at the gate
told nothing that was not foretold
in this room   and on this date

when the stranger turned left from the bridge
along the Fontanka   and knew
the gates by the iron lions
that growled and let him through

Who shadowed him   Lachesis
the Eumenides   knowing what now
I know and do not know   where they
have taken you   and if   But how

gladly I heard his step
on the stair   his touch on the bell
as shy as a boy's fingertip
touching his first girl

He brought me no lilac   no ring
but something more precious than love
As the terrible downpour ceased
he brought me   like Noah's dove

a green word out of the blue
A Russian bird rinsing the air
of its thunder and ash   and if
he flew off   he returned later

and Europe again put out her leaves
behind my Amedeo's head
the drawing on his knee   my wall
Modigliani *famous   dead*

He brought me leaves and he brought
me stone   He brought me Salomé
back from the dim pharaonic vault
of the Stray Dog cabaret

and up   it seemed   the deeper stairs
those others had descended   who
as memory turned the key
came at her shadow   trooping through

the hall   to meet the guest whom I
admitted to the Masquerade
when destiny called the tune
But whose was the tune I played

the music to which we moved
in the candlelight   pouring wine
dividing between us the clutch
of potatoes   your hand and mine

and his hand with a cigar
conducting   Something by Mozart
Donna Anna dreams a dream
Footsteps   and the dreams depart

He brought me leaves and he brought
me stone   a guest of stone
to drag you from the candlelight
Now Donna Anna sits alone

and will do what must be done
if you   in some cage   tonight
are to lie beyond the range
of the poem's fatal flight

Let it be lettered in flame
translated into air
to be printed and reprinted
anytime   anywhere

under roof or under stars
on the one press that survives
the listeners   the watchers
the searchers with their knives.

From the year 1940 I look
  As if down from a tower on it all,
    As if I were taking leave again
      Of all I took leave of long ago,
        As if I had made the sign of the cross
        And went to the vaults below.

                              25 August 1941
                              Leningrad under siege

New Year's Eve. The Fontanny Palace. Instead
of the man expected, shades of 1913 appear to
the author in the shape of mummers. A white hall
of mirrors. Lyrical digression: the Guest from
the Future. A Masquerade. A Poet. A Ghost.

  I have lit my sacred candles
    To halo the New Year,
      And I welcome 1941
        With you who do not appear.

Good God!
              The flames drown in crystal
    'And the wine like poison burns'.
      Rough shards of speech resurface
        As old hysteria returns
And the clock still does not strike . . .
    In mounting anxiety
      Like a shadow on the threshold
        I guard my sanctuary.

I hear a bell's insistent ring
  And feel my blood run colder,
    And turned to stone, ice, fire,
      I look over my shoulder
As if remembering something,
  And in a low voice say:
    'I'm sorry. The Doges' Palace
      Is next door, but today

You might as well leave all
  Your masks and cloaks, your crowns
    And scepters in the hall.
      I've a mind to sing your praises,
        New Year's Eve hell-raisers.'
Here is Faust, and here Don Juan,
  Dapertutto, Iokanaan,
    And here the Nordic Glahn,
      Or the murderer Dorian,
        All of them whispering
          To their Dianas some
            Old Story. One has brought
              A Bacchante with a drum.
And the walls have opened for them,
  Light has erupted, sirens wail,
    The ceiling swells to a dome.
      As if scandal could make me quail . . .
What to me are Hamlet's garters!
  Or the dance of Salomé
    Or the Man in the Iron Mask!
      I am more iron than they . . .
And whose turn now to be afraid,
  To back away, wince guiltily,
    And ask forgiveness for old sins?
      I see:
                What do they want, but me?
Supper was not laid for them,
  And our worlds are not the same.
    Those coat-tails conceal a tail . . .
      How elegant he is, how lame . . .
But . . . surely you have not dared
  To bring the Prince of Darkness here?
    That face or mask or skull
      Displays an anguished sneer
That only Goya would dare paint.
  Prince Charming, Prince Derision –
    Compared with whom, the worst
      Of sinners is a saint . . .
On with the carnival!
  But why am I alone alive?

Tomorrow morning I shall wake
And no indictments will arrive,
And the blue beyond my windows
Will laugh into my face.
But I am frightened; shall go in
Hugging my shawl, my lace,
Smile at them all and say nothing.
I do not want to meet again
This side of Jehosophat
The woman that I was then
In a necklace of black agate.
Can the Last Day be here . . . ?
I have forgotten your lessons,
False prophets of yesteryear,
But you have not forgotten me.
The future in the past draws breath
As the past in the future rots –
Dead leaves in a dance of death.

The sound of invisible feet,
Cigar smoke blue in the air
Over a parquet floor,
And in all the mirrors there
The man who did not appear
And could not enter that hall.
A man much the same as the rest,
The grave had not made his flesh crawl
And there is warmth in his hand –
My Guest from the Future – a light
In his eye. Will he really come,
Turning left from the bridge, tonight?

3

Tonight and every night   the bell
the stove and the candles burn
Before the tocsin tolls again
hell-raisers must return

The stove window reddens
with a city in flames
redoubled in a river
the Moskvá   Nevá   Thames

debouching into Phlegethon

I saw there some up to their eyes in blood
and the great centaur told me   These are the tyrants
who from mass-murder made a livelihood

They choke in the smoking torrents
from springs they unstopped themselves
Napoleon is treading blood
the vintage of 1812

That swastika forelock signals
dreams of a higher race
The blood of jews and gypsies
accuses him to his face

and there is the Children's Friend
islanded in midstream
eyelids   moustache   encrusted
but that is not his scream

Great centaur   shaper of war and peace
what of your argument
that power is the people's will
transferred with their consent

to him   and him   and him   Because
you legitimate their claims
you do your sentry duty
in this abyss of flames

I have called you too a monster
and hated you with all my heart
but in the night of history
you played a homeric part

Under the comet's peacock tail
your city   like Homer's Troy
is still an active volcano
a city flame cannot destroy

a torch by whose shuddering light
you show me what you were shown
a road   a blizzard   prisoners
turned in their sleep to stone

Great centaur   I thought of you
and the prisoners   I thought of them
in the line that shuffled towards
my smouldering Requiem

And so it begins again
the snow starting to fall
At a darkened window I look
as if down from a tower on it all

as if I were taking leave again
of all I took leave of long ago
my son dragged out by a stone guest
a pattern without purpose   No

The pattern must be the shadow
of purpose   by which I know
that my Guest from the Future turned
left from the bridge because Clio

dictated it   she who dictated
the lines on a page of snow
in a wind too cold to let
the tears it loosened flow

preserving them for a future
the past may no longer rot
when spring winds can bear witness
to what the chroniclers do not

The Voice from the Bridge

*For Gail and Zellman Warhaft
and in memory
of Sasha Warhaft
1985-1988*

'All I can hope is that the voice of Kavadias may be
heard, however faintly, from the bridge on a dark
night somewhere in the Indian Ocean.'

Gail Holst Warhaft, translator:
The Collected Poems of Nikos Kavadias

1

*Tonight, as the tropic day drops its sail
and flocks of marabou are flying west,
I'm needled by a need to have it out,
the cancerous secret in my chest.*

*I was a midshipman on a mail-boat line
that did the run from Cairo to Marseilles.
She was a passenger – an Alpine flower –
and soon my friend, my sister you could say.*

*A skinny, sad, aristocratic girl,
whose rich Egyptian father had cut his throat,
she took her sadness on long voyages,
hoping to leave it somewhere, like a coat.*

*She carried Bashkirtsev's Journal about,
regarded Avila's saint with devotion,
recited me mournful poems in French,
and stared for hours at the wide blue ocean.*

*And I, a lost soul, familiar only
with the bodies of whores and the lash of the sea,
listened in ecstasy, as to a saint,
and found a child's joy in her company.*

I gave her a cross to wear round her neck,
she gave me a wallet to ride on my heart.
I was the saddest man in all the world
reaching the port where we had to part.

On cargo boats I used to think of her
as an accomplice, guardian angel, friend.
Her photo in the fo'c'sle was my far
oasis, Ithaca, journey's end.

I should leave it at that. My hand is shaking.
My lungs are inflamed by the scorching air.
Exotic swamp lilies stink to high heaven,
and a stupid marabou's squawking out there.

But I'll go on . . . one tropic night in port,
completely bottled, tankarded, drammed,
I staggered, around midnight, along the road
towards the dirty hovels of the damned.

Disgusting women pulled the sailors in;
one of them, cackling, snatched my cap
(an old French custom of the whores' quarter).
I didn't really want her but chased her up.

A narrow room, as filthy as another,
the plaster peeling from a blistered wall;
she was a rag-doll with a croaking voice,
and dark eyes focused on nothing at all.

She switched the light off and we both went down.
I felt her bones, smelt absinthe on her breath,
her body. And I woke, as poets say,
'When rosy-petalled dawn had strewn the earth'.

Her face was ashen. In the morning light
such pitiful desolation showed
that quickly, as if frightened, I took out
my wallet to pay her what I owed.

Twelve French francs . . . but she gave a sudden cry,
and stared at me like a lunatic –
at me and my wallet. And I froze too
for I had seen the cross around her neck.

Forgetting my cap, I ran like crazy,
gasping, stumbling, but a foul disease
was working in my blood, and even now
it gives me hell at times like these.

The sailors I've served with say of me
I'm a tough sort of bastard and twisted too,
that I don't screw girls and I shoot cocaine.
The buggers wouldn't blame me if they knew.

My hand shakes . . . it's fever . . . I've been distracted,
staring at a motionless marabou
and thinking as he stares back at me
how foolish and lonely: I'm just like you.

2

I heard the voice, but who was speaking?

The radio officer lolls in his chair
and stokes a pipe to carry him past
the Siren's song, 'Le Cimitière

Marin'. He changes course for kinder seas,
where a man can steer by his childhood stars
and every lighthouse beckons him home
to Piraeus – cranes and balconies and bars –

where bead curtains click in a hot wind spiced
with hashish. In the engine room his heart
is running steadily, and at the bow
wave after wave falls apart, falls apart

like an opened book. Hexameters roll
through his head in an older voice, that brings
Odysseus over the wine-dark sea
to the rise and fall of flying-fish wings.

Furrows the oars cut screws reopen.
The radio officer sits in the dark
imagining sailcloth, a tilting plank,
and himself bait for the man-trap shark.

He reddens his pipe, and through the smoke
there comes in a woman who does not speak –
Calypso, the Egyptian – but tonight
I hear a woman's voice speaking not Greek

but English. Marrying her voice to his
in Ithaca (New York), she learns despair
deferred, while keeping watch or studying
the instruments at midnight from his chair.

His odyssey prepares her for her own:
the bright stars blown out one by one,
the straits, the rip-tide, watches, instruments
that monitor the sinking of her son.

The dark is full of voices. Ship to ship
and ship to shore, they throw a line
across the waves, and sometimes they entwine:
Kavadias's, Homer's, hers, and mine.

3

With no Penelope, no Telemachus,
Kavadias wrote ballads in old age
for Philip, his grand-nephew, and I think
he now repays a woman for her language,
delighting her small son with odysseys
until her landfall in their anchorage.

230

'All this takes place on a hilly island in the Mediterranean,' Picasso said. 'Like Crete. That's where the minotaurs live, along the coast. They're the rich *Seigneurs* of the island. They know they're monsters, and they live, like dandies and dilettantes everywhere, the kind of existence that reeks of decadence in houses filled with works of art by the most fashionable painters and sculptors . . . . A minotaur keeps his women lavishly but he reigns by terror and they're glad to see him killed.' . . . He turned to another print, a minotaur watching over a sleeping woman. 'He's studying her, trying to read her thoughts,' he said, 'trying to decide whether she loves him *because* he's a monster.' He looked up at me. 'Women are odd enough for that, you know.' He looked down at the etching again. 'It's hard to say whether he wants to wake her or kill her,' he said.

Françoise Gilot and Carlton Lake: *Life with Picasso*

THE SLEEPING GYPSY

I was the gypsy sleeping
under a desert moon
white-bellied as the mandolin
beside me on the dune.

The wind that stirred my rainbow dress
was no wind but the breath
of some beast with my father's eyes
and the smell of death.

LIBERATION

1

In the room above the studio
he freed me from my dress
and tossing it over a chair
stood back and said 'Yes.

Incredible how accurately
I had prefigured your form.'
Afterwards on the bed,
his touch was warm

but distant: sculptor's hands
about their business find
whether their handiwork
is ready to be signed.

2

Outside the studio,
after dark one could see
boys building barricades;
inside the studio,
after Liberation
the Fruits of Victory –
tinned peaches, hams, one day
a G.I.'s rum ration
and a crate of grenades
inscribed *'To Picasso
from Hemingway.'*

3

After Cézanne's Apples
and with their sculpted weight,
Picasso's Pineapples
shadow a blue-rimmed plate.

Objets Trouvés? Still Life?
Each in its fissured skin
impervious to the knife.
To peel one, pull the pin.

MY LAST MISTRESS

That's my last mistress on the easel. I
call her 'The Fallen Picador' – and why?
She lived ten years with the minotaur
and deserved to leave with the honours of war,
so when Vallauris last July declared
me president of the *corrida*, I shared
the honours with her. Seeing that the bull
was *my* symbol, the horse *her* symbol,
what end could be more fitting than that they
should face each other in a ritual way –
life imitating art, a masterpiece
of living theatre?

       When I took my place
in the president's box and raised my hand,
she was the first out, scattering sand
and with the hooves of her passaging horse
determining my picture's lines of force.
She circled the arena, reined in, bowed
to me as president, and read aloud
the proclamation in my honour. Then
rode from the ring, leaving the bulls and men
to face their deaths. There were no horses killed
that day, but ever since my dreams are filled

with goring. The result you see. Had she
remained, unchanged, the girl who posed for me
in the light of Liberation, hers
would be a face the world remembers,
a daughter of the sun, instead of this
nightmare metamorphosis
of woman into horse: familiar head
and satin flank, the bull's head garlanded
with entrails.

        But enough of her.
Here's something that I fancy you'll prefer –
a necklace. Let me help. Look how your skin
irradiates my metal from within.
It fits that hollow better than its mould,
my bull's horned head Chataganier cast in gold.

The Thread

Burningly it came on me all at once,
This was the place!
   Robert Browning,
      'Childe Roland to the Dark Tower Came'

I was walking as so often on my own,
but nowhere that I knew or wished to be.
There was this desolate plain in front of me.
To left and right, acres of broken stone,
acres of stone behind, and looking down
I saw bare feet under my dimity

and from one heel a brownish thread
stitching stone to stone. I felt no pain,
only a turmoil I could not explain –
a sort of seething in my chest and head,
as if a swarm of bees had nested
in a hollow trunk, and were again

about to swarm. I had no memory,
no notion of how far my feet had still
to go, no will apart from the swarm's will.
I was possessed, and by a mystery
I didn't think to question. I could see
the desert sun was going uphill

and so was I, but didn't see the trees
for the intensity of light
until I was among them: left and right,
an olive grove distorted by disease
or fire into the blackened agonies
of martyrs at the stake. They were all quite

dead, but seemed to clutch at me. Charred arms
were laid on mine, blackened my hands and face,
till suddenly there was this open space,
and I shook like a tree in a storm
without knowing why. The roaring swarm
said with a single voice: 'This is the place.'

There was nothing to see but tumbled rocks
and two far hills like bulls locked horn to horn.
And something else: a huge petrified horn
lay splintered at my feet, between two rocks
that were not rocks, I saw, but finished blocks
of stone. My hands – as if hypnotized – were drawn

to their blunt corners, tugged one and it shifted,
the other and it moved too. Then, with a strength
unrecognizable as mine, I wrenched
each from its socket. The horn I lifted
and laid aside with other dressed stones swiftly
uprooted from a deepening trench.

Some steps, uncovered, led me to a room
brimming with light. My sandals on the floor,
the thread. From that window I first saw –
his head above the rest – the stranger whom
I must forget. I will not think of him.
I put on my sandals and went through the door.

It was all coming back. Perhaps not all,
but rooms behind closed doors came back to me,
a corridor, curtains, a gallery,
and the staircase down to the hall –
the hall now filled with *pithoi* wall to wall,
those man-sized storage jars you see

in the palace at Knossos. Should
I go on? The thread did. Seeing it run
ahead of me, over the flagstones, un-
der the bolted door, suddenly I could
hear what the swarm was saying, understood
what had been done to me, what I had done.

The Naming
For Daphna Erdinast-Vulcan

What's in a name? For you, and now for me,
the echo from a sepia century

of soldiers' boots in a ghetto lane,
pounded doors, the census-taker's refrain:

'What are you?' 'Baker.' 'Tailor.' And the flash
of rabbinical wit – 'I am earth and ash.'

The Women

Did I choose them or did they
choose me, the women who have kept
me company along the way,
women with whom I never slept

but who were with me when I woke
and whispered 'Courage'? Hard
to say who listened and who spoke,
whose voice, whose history I heard.

What did we have in common
except our century?
What drew me to them one by one?
Their kindness – or their fury?

NOTES TO *A FAMILIAR TREE*

p.125   *Old John Young John*. William Pearse, Rector of Preston Bissett 1735-49.

p.126   *To the Honourable Members of the House of Commons*. Preston Bissett was enclosed in 1782.

p.129   *The Birds o' the Parish*. To lease: to glean, pick up ears of corn.

p.131   *William*. The Old Hat public house was built as a canteen for the builders of the present Church of St John the Baptist in the thirteenth century.

p.132   *To Samuel Greatheed, Evangelist*. 'Samuel Greatheed had entered the [Newport Pagnell] Academy as a student in 1785, having previously served with the Army in the corps of engineers in British North America. From being a student he became a tutor in the college, and after ordination assisted in the ministry of the Word in the newly established cause at Woburn. His military service overseas had given him breadth of vision and deep concern for the unevangelised areas of the world, and when the first soundings of the formation of a missionary society were made Greatheed was one of those who made early response. He journeyed to London on horseback to take part in the proceedings at Baker's Chop House which resulted in the foundation of what later came to be known as the London Missionary Society in 1795, and the despatch in the following year of *The Duff*, the first of the long line of ships to sail under the L.M.S. flag, to the South Seas.' Rev. R.G. Martin, *The Chapel 1660-1960: The story of the Congregational Church, Newport Pagnell, Bucks,* Newport Pagnell, 1960, pp. 11-12.

p.132   *News From Home*. At the Aylesbury Commission in January 1831, 44 men and boys were found guilty of the charge of destroying paper-making machinery at High Wycombe the previous November. All were transported, some in the *Eliza* and *Proteus* to Van Dieman's Land, others in the *Eleanor* to New South Wales.

p.134   *The Tuscan*. 'On Wednesday, October 16th, Mr and Mrs Rodgerson, and Mr Stallworthy, appointed to the Marquesan Islands, together with Mr and Mrs Loxton, appointed to Raiatea, one of the

Society Islands, embarked at Gravesend on board the ship *Tuscan*, Captain Stavers, bound for the South Seas.

The Board of Directors gratefully records the sense it entertains of the renewed act of Christian kindness of Alexander Birnie and Son, Esqrs, owners of the ship *Tuscan*, in presenting to the Society a free passage for the missionaries and their wives to the South Sea Islands on board the said ship; also for the gratuitous freight of supplies for the missionary stations in that part of the world.' *Evangelical Magazine*, 1833, p. 510.

p.136   *The Marquesas.* A group of islands 1,500 miles north-east of Tahiti.

p.137   *The Beginning. Atua*: god. *Fafa*: mouth. In Marquesan – as in other Polynesian languages – every vowel is pronounced.

p.138   *The Contest. Marae*: an open space, meeting place. *Tahuata*: one of the Marquesas Islands.

p.139   *23 August 1844.* The Marquesas were annexed by France in 1842.

p.140   *18 December 1847.* Falealili: a village on the island of Upolu, Western Samoa.

p.142   *6 November 1859.* 'It was on the morning of Monday, the 7th inst., that our brother was taken from us. He had gone through his accustomed Sabbath duties as usual. He preached from the words, "Let me die the death of the righteous, and let my last end be like his." This subject was no doubt selected with reference to the death of a native, that had just occurred in Mrs Turner's family. It was remarkable, however, in connection with what was so soon to transpire. His last public service was the administration of the Lord's Supper, at which he gave an address from the words, "I will smite the shepherd, and the sheep of the flock shall be scattered abroad," words regarded by the students of the Institution as of ominous import in the present weakened state of our Mission. On the previous Sabbath he had preached from words equally remarkable: "Come, Lord Jesus; come quickly." It would seem as if his mind had been led to those very themes which we may conceive he would have chosen had he known that the coming of the Lord to him was indeed at hand.' Letter dated 11 November 1859 from A.W. Murray to the Rev. Dr. Tidman, the Foreign Secretary of the L.M.S., *Evangelical Magazine*, 1860, p. 284.

p.144   *20 December 1859.* Rarotonga: one of the Cook Islands.

p.146   *The Arrival.* Rolling Road: a broad track, thirty to forty feet wide, in which every advantage is taken of the natural incline of the land, and from which all trees have been removed, the stumps cut level with the surface, and large holes filled up. The kauri trunks are manhandled along these tracks until they reach the water.

Timber jack: a simple mechanical device for 'jacking up' and rolling kauri logs.

The Circular: a large circular saw.

p.150 *With a Copy of* Early Northern Wairoa. A work of local history, *Early Northern Wairoa*, was written by John Stallworthy, formerly M.P. for Kaipara, and printed at the Wairoa Bell & Northern Advertiser Printing Works, Dargaville, 1916.

p.150. *A Couple of Field Postcards/1919.* 'Another crusade fizzled out after the war. The teetotallers almost succeeded, in 1919, in winning their campaign. Only the votes of the Servicemen overseas, 90 per cent of whom voted "wet", saved the New Zealanders from that unlawful thirst which tantalized the Americans in the twenties.' Keith Sinclair, *A History of New Zealand*, O.U.P., 1961.

p.151 *Congratulations.* Section: the sections, plots of land, awarded to returning veterans of the Great War were sometimes of poor quality and a cause of subsequent resentment.

p.162 *One for the Road.* Red Devilment/free-falling . . . : the Red Devils are the Parachute Regiment's team of free-fall parachutists.

p.163 'Mirror for a Prince'; *Beowulf* is thought by some to be an early example of the 'Prince's Mirror', a tradition later to include such other works of instruction for young noblemen as Machiavelli's *The Prince* and Castiglione's *The Courtier*.

THE BARE BONES OF THE TREE

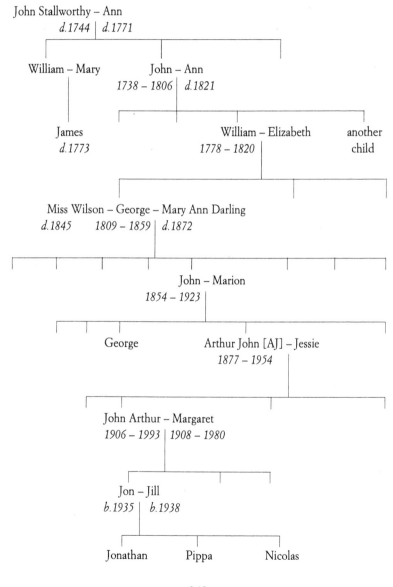

John Stallworthy – Ann
d.1744 | *d.1771*

William – Mary
John – Ann
1738 – 1806 | *d.1821*

James
d.1773
William – Elizabeth
1778 – 1820
another
child

Miss Wilson – George – Mary Ann Darling
d.1845 *1809 – 1859* | *d.1872*

John – Marion
1854 – 1923

George
Arthur John [AJ] – Jessie
1877 – 1954

John Arthur – Margaret
1906 – 1993 | *1908 – 1980*

Jon – Jill
b.1935 | *b.1938*

Jonathan   Pippa   Nicolas

INDEX OF FIRST LINES

a black thread   91
A feature of the guest-house window   22
A GOLD LOCKET lost in the street   103
A house without a man   133
A man in his shirtsleeves   108
A poem is   11
A refugee finds refuge: San   74
A rose is not a rose   59
After an amputation, he had heard   36
After the hot convulsion, this   190
All I could hear when he stiffened and listened   102
All that Anglo-Saxon jazz   76
All the way to the hospital   158
and a house of more books than bricks   56
Another harvest gathered in   114
Another time,   173
As I was crossing Trafalgar Square   72
As the mad woman cried out in the square,   40
As the wheels on the hearse   169
Asleep till nine, again you break   36
At midday the tree   116
At 40,000 feet   105
At sundown, two dolphins   103
At the end of the road, in a drab chapel   172

Barefoot through the bazaar,   42
Bells   dinting the afternoon   131
Between   32
Between the decorous lips   169
Black window opposite   94
Bowing and scraping   the notary's pen: 128

City pigeons on the air   60
'Cognac – more cognac for Monsieur Lautrec –   39

Counsel yourself that traveller   36

Dear Dad,   150
Dear Dad,   154
Dear God,   148
Dear John, if a sinner may so   123
Dear Johnny,   145
Dear Marion,   147
Dear Nick,   162
Did I choose them or did they   238

Father,   148
First of the migrants, overnight they say   45
From Gravesend on the morning tide.   136
From W.B. Yeats to his friend Maud Gonne.   38

God made the first – in a dreamwork-shop   184
Good Master Greatheed,   132
Good on you, Doctor John!   151

Half grown before half seen,   65
He at the sill saying   64
He looks up, wondering why   119
He went to the cinema; saw   51
He with his puppet, I with my *Testament*   138
His pen – his journal – but   143
Hugging his dolphin, our stone boy stands   115
Hush-a-bye-baby   on the tree top   124

'I am the capital', head says,   106
I do not know much about love, but I know   53
I have been there again, and seen the backs   110
I made my son a poem   186
I owe you an apology,   101
I was the gypsy sleeping   231
I was walking as so often on my own,   235
In their grandmothers' footsteps, the girls   192
indigo skies   105
It was. The breech smelling of oil,   28

Leader of insurgents he knew too much   79
Leather and wood and stone –   68
Light is come amongst them, but they   139
Lighter by a life, you settle back   118
Little fox, little fox, with your brush of hair,   17
Lying in late: 102

Margaret, born to the flawless summers   187
Mid-day, mid-summer   107
Mile after dark Silesian mile   210
Miss Lavender taught us to ride   29
My dear,   82
My dear George,   150
My dear Mother,   146
My dear uncle,   134
My father in his study sits up late,   64
My nephew,   132
My story? Yes, I got my story   201

No longer when the lights flick on   70
No ordinary Sunday. First the light   30
Now that the chestnut candles burn   91

O do not let the levelling sea,   15
October, and I learn   85
of one who grew up at Gallipoli   31
On one side of the world   180
On the ground floor the wealthy and their cats   53
On the wall above the basins in the barber's shop   44
Only the wind was up before me   136
Open the window, let in the wind   117
Out of the silence   181
Out of what depths the dream?   193

panther-footed saunter in the street,   50
Passing the great plane tree in the square –   110
Prince of my blood, the swifts have flown   163

Reading you the story you cannot understand   118
remembers the red   114

Returning to the biscuit tin   167
'Ritual' is perhaps too large a word: 52
'Roast chestnuts, a shilling   93
Rounding the Horn, such seas!   152

Satchel on hip   58
She finding on his lips   63
Sirs: 126
Snow inexhaustibly   75
So much in common being not enough   99
So, you have noticed: I am not   156
soon to be ripped   183
Spring come early, spring come late,   129

Take 1 green pepper and 2 tomatoes   99
Taking me into your body   101
Taking my evening walk   62
Thank you, Matisse,   98
The bird that dropped the cherry stone   185
The boys wink at the boys: 'Here comes Sir George.'   48
The chapel silent and the candles weeping.   20
The cry and the silence   67
The day my father stayed in bed   125
The doorbell   a tocsin   tolling   220
'The finest blades in Rome',   154
The first night that the monster lurched   41
The four greys fidget as a torch-boy runs   48
The Garden Member with the walking stick   45
The gown on the back of the door –   168
The last morning as an immortal   167
The Peshawar Vale Hunt has gone to ground.   49
The red lights running my way   70
The spotlights you had covered [*thunder*   78
The stone   66
The swimming pool by night in summer   47
The truth, the whole truth always   57
The weathercock once again heading south   119
The willows are gold again   106
The Word was god. God: *Atua.*   137
The world was flat, lawn without end,   27

There are stars in the grass, 184
There was a captain who, weary of land, 18
They are building a road out of Kathmandu – 74
They come together again, 104
This dying of the dog, now gone to earth 22
Though come down in the world to pulling a cart 43
Those cherubs on the gate 83
Those daisies know too much! 105
Three eyes in the mirror 77
Tom – and in time! I never thought you'd come 190
Tonight, as the tropic day drops its sail 227
Tonight, seen through plate-glass 92

Waiting so patiently for Mr Right 52
Walking – but you not with me – round 16
We call them ours, the leaves we saw – 112
We stop in front of the case 109
Well, my colossus, how do things look 80
What's in a name? For you, and now for me, 237
When the chrysalis broke 61
When wing to wing, feather by feather 188
Who disinherits 69
Why, when my head was filled 15
Wicks balance flame, a dark dew falls 44
Words, words, you and your damn 109

Yellow and poster-striped the hornet vans 61
You blame me that I do not write 19
You turn to the window for the first time. 67